Relevant, practical, and grounded in Scripture, this book is a must read for those rebuilding after their world has been turned upside down. It is obvious that Dan writes both from the heart, and years of ministering to the wounded on the front lines of suffering. This book meets the hurting in their darkest hour while inspiring them to reach out in hope for the sometimes unseen hand of God who promises to be there.

> Kevin Ellers, D.Min.
> Territorial Disaster Services Coordinator
> The Salvation Army Central Territory

Broken Dreams, Shattered Lives is a wonderfully developed book outlining a series of steps that will let hurt people find healing. Dan Hurst does an outstanding job in showing from the Scriptures how God's wonderful promises can rebuild your life! If you've been saddened, devastated by a loss, overcome by fear, dealt with a medical illness, or felt abandoned by life, this book can help you put your life back on track. A must-read!

> Dr. Kevin Hubbard
> Heartland Hematology/Oncology Associates

D0280191

Dan Hurst's straight forward to the point writing of Broken Dreams, Shattered Lives will help you step by step as you pick up the pieces of a shattered life. This is a guide for you as you wrestle with your own situation or help someone else. Write questions and statements in the margin as you read, and keep going. BDSL will help you find meaning, discovery and answers in your journey.

Andrea Bergfield, M.A.
Marriage and Family Counseling

It's no secret to any of us that life, in general, is fraught with unique challenges, unexpected changes and unanticipated, life-altering situations. In this book, Dan Hurst, utilizes his unique skill as a gifted student and communicator of the Bible to provide us with a captivating and in-depth look into the heart of God, offering step-by-step solutions that provide healing, peace and resolve. I strongly encourage everyone who has ever asked the question "Why, God?" to read and capture the awesome truths found within the pages of this book, and in spite of the pain or confusion you are experiencing right now, discover the path to the life God has always intended you to have!

Randy Shepard, Ph.D.
President, The Financial Advisory Group

Broken Dreams, Shattered Lives

Putting Life Back Together

Dan Hurst

Be merciful to me, O LORD, for I am in distress; my eyes grow weak with sorrow, my soul and my body with grief. My life is consumed by anguish and my years by groaning; my strength fails because of my affliction, and my bones grow weak. Because of all my enemies, I am the utter contempt of my neighbors; I am a dread to my friends—those who see me on the street flee from me. I am forgotten by them as though I were dead; I have become like broken pottery. For I hear the slander of many; there is terror on every side; they conspire against me and plot to take my life. But I trust in you, O LORD; I say, "You are my God."

Psalm 31:9–14

www.LivingPower.com
(660) 851-1510

Acknowledgements

It is impossible to write and teach successfully without five key things: a calling, a leading, a passion, an opportunity, and an influence. The influences on my life have been overwhelming. Above all I am thankful to God, who saw fit to pour out grace and mercy on me, and to put some amazing people in my life.

I am so deeply grateful to Marcia, the most exceptional wife that God might give a man. To Eric, Jared, and Jordan, the three sons God placed in my life to raise and to teach me joy and hope; to The Open Class Bible Study, the most encouraging and faith-building group of people I've ever encountered; to Angie Kiesling, editor; Charles Joyner, editor; and to Harold Hurst, my dad, my hero, who taught me by example that a life used by God is a life well lived, I say thank you!

O LORD, do not rebuke me in your anger or discipline me in your wrath.

Be merciful to me, LORD, for I am faint; O LORD, heal me, for my bones are in agony.

My soul is in anguish. How long, O LORD, how long?

Turn, O LORD, and deliver me; save me because of your unfailing love.

No one remembers you when he is dead. Who praises you from the grave?

I am worn out from groaning; all night long I flood my bed with weeping and drench my couch with tears.

My eyes grow weak with sorrow; they fail because of all my foes.

Away from me, all you who do evil, for the LORD has heard my weeping.

The LORD has heard my cry for mercy; the LORD accepts my prayer.

All my enemies will be ashamed and dismayed; they will turn back in sudden disgrace.

Psalm 6

Table of Contents

Introduction

I often wonder if God births us with a lump in His throat, knowing what we're going to have to go through.

The call came about midnight.

Her husband, who had been missing for two days, had been found slumped over in the front seat of his car in a downtown parking lot. The conclusion from the autopsy was heart failure. He was diabetic, and the theory was that his blood sugar had dropped and he became disoriented and pulled into the parking lot on his way home from work.

She and her three children would never be the same.

As we made plans for the funeral, it occurred to me that while a funeral is a time to bring a conclusion to a life on earth, it is also a time to face the future and begin rebuilding a life.

Lives can be rebuilt.

It is a truth taught over and over throughout the Bible. We are given so many examples of lives that were shattered—and then restored by God. Lives that were destroyed by sin, deceit, unfaithfulness, lies, disease, war, and loss. Sometimes people caused their own demise. Sometimes they were the victims of someone else's cruelty and sin. Sometimes lives were changed by the natural course of life.

But lives can be rebuilt.

That's what this book is about. I've chosen not to dwell on each subject matter but simply to present it and let you mull it over and come to your own discovery. It won't take very long to read this book, but it will take some time to absorb and begin applying its message. So read it. Mark it up. Make notes to yourself. Challenge it. Question it. Even argue with it. Soon you'll discover that God is still at work in your life, and He's ready to pick up the pieces and put you back together again.

Have you ever been fired from a job? I have. It hurts. Especially if it was done by an unprincipled boss who seemed to enjoy hurting people and their families. I was a victim of that sort of person. It devastated me and my family. It turned our lives upside down. However, God was faithful. He brought my family through the crisis. Most importantly, God rebuilt my life.

I'm here to tell you that the principles in this book work.

Years ago when I was in college, I worked at a small Christian radio station. During my shift a program aired from a radio preacher who would always end his half-hour with "You don't have any problems. All you need is God."

I thought then and still do that it was one of the oddest statements I'd ever heard from a preacher. I mean, if you don't have any problems, why would you need God?

The fact is we have loads of problems. Sometimes they are so overwhelming we're devastated by them. Sometimes our lives fall apart. We need God.

If that's where you are, this book was written for you.

A point of clarification is in order here. These principles are for followers of Jesus Christ. They are based on the Bible and are applicable to those who seek to be what God desires them to be.

Your situation may require professional counseling. Don't shy away from that. God uses counselors in our lives. Read the fifth chapter of 1 Timothy to see that. But know that real healing and health come from God. A counselor who believes and practices that is invaluable.

Whether the crisis or conflict you are going through is based on current events or past events in your life, God knows and has a plan for your life that rises above what you are going through.

My prayer is that through the discovery of these principles, you will find a renewed hope and a restored life.

What Is Going On?

"I felt like I couldn't breathe. I felt claustrophobic, like I was going to be sick. Here I had just bought a house, my wife was home with a new baby, and my company told me that I was being terminated immediately with two weeks' severance pay. And the only thing I could think was, 'What do I do now?'"

Those are the words of a friend of mine who lost his job a couple of months ago. He lost a job making six figures with benefits and is now working a retail job making only 15 percent of what he formerly made, with no benefits.

- - - -

"It all happened so fast! He went to the doctor for his acid reflux and a few days later we got the report that he had cancer. He hadn't even felt that bad. And three months later he was gone. How

does that happen to someone who was never sick? Now I'm left with a pile of bills and two little boys to take care of. I just feel lost. I have no idea what I should do next."

What would you say to a young woman who lost the love of her life and has no answers about her future? Somehow a simple prayer and a Scripture verse aren't enough.

- - - -

"Yes, I got caught. Yes, I committed a crime. Yes, I'm deeply sorry for what I did. Do I deserve twenty years in jail for it? I don't think so. Lots of other people have done far worse with far fewer consequences. This really isn't fair. But what am I going to do? I'm here and it's not going to change. And if I survive sixteen more years I'll be a free man. Broken, but free."

Sometimes we're the victim. Sometimes we're the culprit. But in either case life changes. It's not over, but it definitely changes.

- - - -

"The police say he fell asleep at the wheel. We had just talked to him about four hours before. He was so relieved finals were over and he could come home for the winter break. He was so excited that

he was going to be able to get together with some of his friends that were away at other colleges. But just five miles from home he must have nodded off and lost control of the car. I really don't even want to go on anymore."

What possible words of comfort can you give to parents who have lost a child?

- - - -

"He just walked out on me. He said he couldn't go on with the lie anymore, that he didn't really love me the way I needed to be loved, and he walked out. And that was it. It was over. I don't even know what really happened."

Life can be so confusing...and so unfair, especially when someone betrays our trust and love.

- - - -

"It's so unfair. I was molested as a child. I've lived silently with it ever since. He went on with his life, but I've had trouble trusting people ever since. Why am I the one that suffers for it?"

Does God really know what happened to you? Does He care? Can you really get past it?

- - - -

"I had been in Vietnam for six months. I took a mine blast and lost both of my legs. I remember lying in a ditch thinking I've got to survive, and at the same time thinking I don't want to spend the rest of my life like this. So now I'm in a wheelchair. I can't work. I'm pretty much a waste of skin."

Does God give up on people like this? Does He still have a purpose and a plan? Is He to blame, or is He to trust?

- - - -

I've been in the ministry for over thirty years, and I can tell you that everyone – everyone – goes through crisis, loss, and brokenness. There are times in our lives when we are so overwhelmed by emotional or physical pain that life just doesn't seem worth it.

In spite of what it may seem like right now, God does have a plan and a purpose for your life that isn't destroyed or even deterred by what you're going through. That remarkable truth is backed up over and over in His Word.

> *I know that you can do all things; no plan of yours can be thwarted.*
>
> Job 42:2

Here's something else you need to know: God thinks bigger than you do.

Picture a large white wall. I walk up to the wall and with my pen draw a very, very small speck in the middle of it. You wonder what I'm up to, but you focus on the speck.

You don't see the immensity of the white wall compared to the speck. All you notice is the black spot.

We tend to look at the dark spots in our lives and miss how much white space there is. Now I'm not suggesting that the dark spot should be ignored. It can't be. It shouldn't be. But we do need to look at it in the context of the huge white wall.

We get focused on an infinitesimally small part of life compared to eternity. But God sees beyond the dark spot. He sees what is happening in this dark spot to prepare you for eternity.

You are an eternal being. God created you that way. No man has ever lived his life on earth and then died, and that was it. Life is eternal. God designed it that way.

The body you are living in is not eternal, but the "you" in that body is. God has eternal plans for you that reach far beyond this dark spot in your life.

God is preparing you for eternity!

Doesn't it make sense that if we are going to live for eternity we are going to have things to do for eternity? Do you think God created the vastness of space with all its millions of galaxies and solar systems without a plan and a purpose? Doesn't it make sense that the intricacies of life factor into that?

God has not left anything to chance. He has, by design, left many things to choice, but not to chance. But here's some good news: God knew about this issue in your life way before you did. In fact, He knew about it before He even created your life.

> *My frame was not hidden from you when I was made in the secret place. When I was woven together in the depths of the earth, your eyes saw my unformed body. All the days ordained for me were written in your book before one of them came to be.*
>
> Psalm 139:15–16

In the prophet Jeremiah's case, God made it very clear that before we're born He has designs on our life.

> *Before I formed you in the womb I knew you, before you were born I set you apart...*
>
> Jeremiah 1:5

So if God has a plan and a purpose for your life, this thing that has devastated your life is not a surprise to Him. Nor does it change His goal for your life.

If God has a plan and a purpose for your life, this thing that has devastated your life is not a surprise to Him. Nor does it change His goal for your life.

God made it very clear that He planned you before He even created the earth.

> *For he chose us in him before the creation of the world to be holy and blameless in his sight.*
>
> Ephesians 1:4

Now, if God planned you before the beginning of the earth, He's not going to let this devastation in your life change His plans. In His infinite knowledge, power, and wisdom He can somehow use this matter or overcome it to accomplish His plan. That's not to say He's insensitive, uncaring, unloving, or even wanted it to happen.

We wonder why bad things happen to good people. But why is that God's fault?

The first chapter of Genesis clearly states that God gave man responsibility to manage the earth. The third chapter of Genesis paints the reality of man's failure and sin.

The bottom line is that man is responsible for the sin and failure in the world. Not God. Over and over, it has been man's failure to obey God that brought about the consequences of sin. You have to blame man for sin and its consequences in the world. And man will give account for his failure.

Nothing in all creation is hidden from God's sight. Everything is uncovered and laid bare before the eyes of him to whom we must give account.

Hebrews 4:13

Don't blame God for your crisis. He didn't cause it. Blame the person responsible. Nor should you assume that God is punishing you for something. This is important to understand. There is a huge difference between punishment and discipline.

Punishment is retribution for something. Punishment is a judgment, a judgment for something that deserves an equal response to the severity of the action being judged.

That's why Jesus died on the cross. In His love for you, as His own creation, He took the punishment for your sin. So it makes no sense that God is punishing you. He already took your place – your punishment – for you. And that loving forgiveness is available to you if you'll go to God for it.

No, you are not being punished. More than likely you are suffering one of two things: the consequences of your own sin, which brings about discipline, or the consequences of someone else's sin (even if it was Adam's sin as explained in 1 Corinthians 15:22).

If it is the consequences of someone else's sin, there is nothing else that seems so unjust or so unfair. Whether it is something that happened years ago and still haunts you, or something that you are going through right now, there is good news. God knows exactly what happened, He hasn't forgotten you, and He is still at work preparing your life for eternity. You have suffered something incomprehensible to most people, but God wants you to know two things.

First, He offers you grace. Grace is best defined as "the divine influence on the heart and its reflection in life." God doesn't want you to just "tough it out" or ignore what happened to you. He wants to bring a divine influence into your life that will reflect through your life.

The second thing God wants you to know is that He offers you hope.

I don't want to get into that here because we'll deal with that in Principle 6, but hope is a life changer. It is one of the most misunderstood words in the Bible. It is such a powerful influence that the apostle Paul categorized it with faith and love in 1 Corinthians 13:13.

On the other hand, if what you are going through is the result of your own choices, it may be a discipline in your life.

Here's the difference between punishment and discipline: as I mentioned, punishment is retribution for something. However, discipline is getting you to do the right thing.

One of my favorite stories in the Bible is the story of Jonah.

It's odd that it's one of my favorite stories because, frankly, I don't like Jonah. He was a self-centered, mouthy, petulant brat. If it had been up to me, I would have punished him. But God chose to discipline him – He chose to do what He had to do to get Jonah to do the right thing.

This is critical to understand. You aren't being punished for something. As we've seen, God the Father already did that to Jesus on the cross on your behalf. But it is possible that God is doing what He has to do to get you to do what He wants you to do. The fact is that God is at work in your life to renew and revitalize you for His purposes.

But what if this dark time in your life isn't someone else's fault, or even your fault? Take for example the loss of a loved one. Sometimes we struggle because of the natural course of life.

It doesn't seem like it right now, but God is up to something in your life. He has not abandoned you. He's more at work now than you can even imagine!

How do I know that?

Because the Bible is very clear that God is at work in the needs of your life.

Let us then approach the throne of grace with confidence, so that we may receive mercy and find grace to help us in our time of need.

Hebrews 4:16

His divine power has given us every-thing we need for life and godliness through our knowledge of him who called us by his own glory and good-ness.

2 Peter 1:3

And my God will meet all your needs according to his glorious riches in Christ Jesus.

Philippians 4:19

God is at work where there are needs. That's what He does. That's how He works. God is up to something in your life!

The fact that you have such a heavy need in your life is a sure sign that God is doing some-thing to prepare you for His eternal purpose and plan! He's using this issue in your life to shape you into what He has planned for eter-nity!

Here is something that you can anchor your life on:

Everything that happens to you is either allowed by God or engineered by God.

That seems to be a rather harsh and simplified statement, but think about it. God is looking at the big wall of eternity. If in this small dark spot of your life He can shape you more into what He wants to accomplish through you, it will be worth it!

With that in mind, here are eleven things to do to put your life back together.

Principle #1
Don't Be Afraid

Before you go any further, answer these three questions:

- What's your purpose in life? In other words, what do you believe you were created for? What do you believe God wants to accomplish through you?
- What is your primary goal in life, the number one priority to accomplish before you die?
- What is your greatest fear in life? It's important that you dig deep for this one. Keep asking yourself "why?" until you get down to the root fear.

Now set those answers aside for a few minutes and let's take a look at one of the greatest Bible heroes: Abraham. The following story in the Bible takes place shortly after Abraham has been introduced. Does this impress you as someone who is one of God's trophies?

> *Then Abram set out and continued toward the Negev. Now there was a famine in the land, and Abram went down to Egypt to live there for a while because the famine was severe. As he was about to enter Egypt, he said to his wife Sarai, "I know what a beautiful woman you are. When the Egyptians see you, they will say, 'This is his wife.' Then they will kill me but will let you live. Say you are my sister, so that I will be treated well for your sake and my life will be spared because of you." When Abram came to Egypt, the Egyptians saw that she was a very beautiful woman. And when Pharaoh's officials saw her, they praised her to Pharaoh, and she was taken into his palace. He treated Abram well for her sake, and Abram acquired sheep and cattle, male and female donkeys, menservants and maidservants, and camels. But the LORD inflicted serious diseases on Pharaoh and his household because*

of Abram's wife Sarai. So Pharaoh summoned Abram. "What have you done to me?" he said. "Why didn't you tell me she was your wife? Why did you say, 'She is my sister,' so that I took her to be my wife? Now then, here is your wife. Take her and go!" Then Pharaoh gave orders about Abram to his men, and they sent him on his way, with his wife and everything he had.

Genesis 12:9–20

Abraham had a problem. In spite of the fact that he believed God, obeyed God, worshipped God, and generally trusted God, he still had a problem. He sometimes operated out of fear.

In Genesis 20 he pulled this very same stunt with King Abimelech. And the implication is that he had done this several times.

Before you judge Abraham, think about your own life. When you make choices because of your fear, you make wrong choices.

This is critical to understand. If you are operating out of fear right now because of your life's circumstances, you are going to make the wrong decisions.

Remember the three questions at the beginning of this chapter?

When you make choices because of your fear, you make wrong choices.

- What is your purpose in life?
- What is your goal in life?
- What is your greatest fear?

Let's take a look at how your answers to those questions factor into your current situation.

This analysis is based on the world's way of doing things. As Christians we have to draw different conclusions because we have the work of the Holy Spirit in our lives, but in our weak moments, these worldly principles tend to direct us.

People generally believe that the way they accomplish their purpose in life is by reaching their goal in life. For example, if your purpose in life is to be happy, and your goal is to be independently wealthy, you tend to think that independent wealth is the way to happiness.

Let's draw another scenario.

If your purpose in life is to get to heaven and your goal in life is to "be fulfilled," then it's a pretty easy conclusion that you tend to think personal fulfillment (however you define that) is the way to heaven.

However, the reality is that for most people their goal in life is to avoid their greatest fear!

If your fear is rejection, and your goal is to be independently wealthy, then you probably feel that the way you avoid rejection is by being independently wealthy.

If your fear is death, and your goal is to be personally fulfilled, then you probably feel that the way to avoid whatever it is you fear about death is by being personally fulfilled.

What it boils down to is that most people operate out of fear. They make choices and plans based on their fear. They build their life around avoiding their fear.

When you ask people what their greatest fear is you get some interesting answers. These were some individual answers given in an online survey:

> *"My greatest fear in my life is losing my job. I have way too many bills. If I lost my job I would lose everything."*

> *"My greatest fear in life is failure. I fear messing up so bad as a mother that I ruin my kids. And I fear that when I look back on my life I'll have some awful regrets. I already regret leaving my husband, but I don't know what else I could have done."*

> *"My greatest fear is that my life will be insignificant."*

"I have several fears, but they're all related. When my son lived at home I was so afraid for my life because I knew he was a drug addict, and I was afraid the police were going to come and take him away. Now that he's away from home I fear that in his irresponsibility he'll drive under the influence and kill someone. I fear that because of his drugs he'll go to jail for the rest of his life. I fear that I'll go broke because of his irresponsibility, and I'll have nothing for my retirement."

Do you see how debilitating and life-consuming fear is? Fear seems to fall into two general categories: death and/or rejection.

Fear of Death

This fear reveals itself a number of different ways, including:

- *Fear of Pain.* For example, a fear of dying a slow and painful death.
- *Fear of Failure.* For example, a fear of dying as a failure or being remembered as a failure.

- ***Fear of Loss of Control.*** This is a fear of losing control of one's life.

But God has something amazing to say about this sort of fear.

> *So we say with confidence, "The Lord is my helper; I will not be afraid...."*
>   Hebrews 13:6

This is such an encouraging verse, especially when you understand what the word "helper" means.

The Greek word used is actually made up of two words. One word means "a cry for help." The other word means "to run." The word picture is that "the Lord runs to me when He hears me cry for help."

What an encouraging and sustaining truth this is. God runs to you when He hears you cry, just as a parent runs to a child's side when the child cries out.

How can you overcome your fear of death? By getting to know personally and intimately the one who overcame death!

> *Since the children have flesh and blood, he too shared in their humanity so that by his death he might destroy him who holds the power of*

*death—that is, the devil—and free
those who all their lives were held in
slavery by their fear of death.*

Hebrews 2:15

The Bible implies that Abraham eventually overcame his fear of death. The story is told in Genesis 20. It's the second time the Bible records Abraham telling Sarah to say that he was her brother. King Abimelech figured it out and confronted him. Abraham confessed to it, and apparently he got right with God on the matter.

There is something very important I want you to see here. One of the other significant problems in Abraham's life was that Sarah was barren. It must have puzzled Abraham how God could promise that he would be the father of a great nation, but Sarah couldn't have children.

After Abraham deals with his fear and prays at the end of chapter 20, look how chapter 21 starts:

Now the LORD was gracious to Sarah as he had said, and the LORD did for Sarah what he had promised. Sarah became pregnant and bore a son to Abraham in his old age, at the very time God had promised him.

Genesis 21:1–2

God is greater than your fear! When you choose (and it is a choice) to do things God's way, you will find victory over the fear that controls you.

Fear of Rejection

The apostle Paul suffered from this sort of fear.

> *I came to you in weakness and fear,*
> *and with much trembling.*
> 1 Corinthians 2:3

I know this category well! I have caught myself operating from this fear so many times. It's such a twisted condition. On the one hand I may want someone or some group of people to accept me, yet on the other hand I know there are unacceptable things about me that are worth rejecting.

So what do I do? I begin filtering what I want them to know or see. I begin to scheme to get them to not reject me. Then suddenly it hits me. This is just one more reason why they should reject me!

It's interesting how many people who are driven by fear of rejection are so motivated to please others.

This fear reveals itself a number of different ways, including:

- *Fear of Failure.* If I fail, I won't be accepted.

So many people are focused on this fear. For them, failure is not an option so they push themselves and the people around them to whatever it is they consider successful. It's a dangerous fear because it puts the plan ahead of the people. You see this a lot in business.

I spent a few years working in radio. For part of that time I had a boss who would jokingly say to the staff, "Your feelings are of no concern to me until the ratings come out."

We all laughed about it, but at the same time we knew there was some truth to it.

One of the biggest dangers of this fear is that it can cause one to have such tunnel-vision they don't see the big picture and therefore are closed to other options and plans.

Fear of failure sends many people over the edge. Unfortunately they sometimes hurt innocent people in the process, all because they are operating out of a fear of failure.

- *Fear of Loss.* If I lose what I have, people will think less of me.

What is it that causes us to think people equate us with what we have? Jesus warned us about that:

And do not set your heart on what you will eat or drink; do not worry about it. For the pagan world runs after all such things, and your Father knows that you need them. But seek his kingdom, and these things will be given to you as well. Do not be afraid, little flock, for your Father has been pleased to give you the kingdom. Sell your possessions and give to the poor. Provide purses for yourselves that will not wear out, a treasure in heaven that will not be exhausted, where no thief comes near and no moth destroys. For where your treasure is, there your heart will be also.

Luke 12:29–34

- *Fear of Loneliness*. If I'm lonely it's because people don't want me or like me.

- *Fear of Meaninglessness*. This is a fear that your life has no meaning, or that your life has no value. Nothing could be further from the truth. God designed you. He destined you. He determined long before you came into existence that you fit into His intricate plan for life.

You are worthy, our Lord and God, to receive glory and honor and power, for you created all things, and by your will they were created and have their being.

Revelation 4:11

I want you to see something very important about this verse. This is part of a worship experience in heaven. In other words, it is something that is clear to the worshippers now that they are in heaven.

It may not have been completely clear on earth, but once they were in heaven and understood more of God's plan their eyes were opened and they worshipped out of a new sense of discovery.

There are two key things we need to glean from this. First, God is worthy of all that we have to offer Him. Second, God created you for His purpose and plan, and you are fulfilled only within that destiny! You are not fulfilled by your plans, but by His.

That truth is revealed to us by God in His Word to help us understand a little more of what He's up to in our lives. It's an encouragement that what we are learning and discovering here on earth will make a whole lot more sense someday. And this part is really important: it will cause us to worship Him!

Think about that. In spite of what you're going through here on earth, someday you will be able to say, *"You are worthy, O Lord, to receive glory and honor and power, for You created all things, and You used all that I am, all that I learned, and all that I experienced to shape me into what YOU wanted. And somehow, in spite of the things that went wrong in my life, You accomplished Your purpose!"*

The conclusion we can draw is that since God is in control, we don't need to fear.

The number one command given in the Bible is "Do not be afraid." That term is stated over sixty times, far more than any other command. If it's that important, you need to pay attention to it!

So how can you overcome your fear?

There are four things you need to discover and apply in your life right away.

- **Realize that fear is not from God.**

  For God did not give us a spirit of timidity [fear], but a spirit of power, of love and of self-discipline.

  2 Timothy 1:7

- **Discover the father-child relationship that God wants to have with you.**

The number one command given in the Bible is "Do not be afraid."

> *For you did not receive a spirit that*
> *makes you a slave again to fear, but*
> *you received the Spirit of sonship.*
> *And by him we cry, "Abba, Father."*
>
> Romans 8:15

Have you ever noticed how a very young child acts around someone they don't know? Usually they are very shy and cautious. As they are around this new person more and more they start to warm up to them. They will try a few experiments to see if they can trust this person.

That's the way we act until we learn to trust God. We mistrust Him even though we want to trust Him, because we don't know Him well enough.

Then, little by little, we try a few things to see if we can trust God, and as God gains our trust, we learn to trust Him for greater things.

Eventually you begin not only to trust God but to obey Him. As your faith in Him grows, you find your fear dissipating. And it doesn't take long for God's love for you and your love for God to overcome fear.

- **Learn to trust God.**

> *When I am afraid, I will trust in*
> *you. In God, whose word I praise,*

in God I trust; I will not be afraid.
What can mortal man do to me?

Psalm 56:3–4

If you are having difficulty trusting God, start by remembering how He brought you through other difficult times—maybe times when you didn't even sense that God was at work.

Get into His Word and find reason to worship and praise Him. Discover how big your God really is! Share in the joy of discovery that so many people in the Bible experienced as they learned to trust God.

- **Fall in love with God.**

How does that happen? It begins by letting God fill your life with Himself. He is "perfect love," and as He takes more and more control of your life, His presence will replace the fear that has been punishing you.

The more you get to know Him, the more you will love Him, because you will sense and understand His love for you. The more you see and believe that He has a purpose and a plan for your life, the more you will trust Him and love Him... and lose your fear.

Dear God,
My fear has so weakened me, even paralyzed me. I've made some choices and decisions by fear. I look at my life and I'm afraid. God, I don't want to operate out of fear. I'm asking You to come into my life and break the bondage of fear that grips me. Set me free to trust You. Fill me with Your power, and love, and self-discipline.

Amen

Principle #2
Rebuild Your Mind

When you've gone through a life-shattering experience, all of your focus and energy is on that crisis. The event controls your thoughts and emotions. It's time to reprogram your mind to a healthy perspective of life and purpose. That can happen through a fresh discovery of what God is up to.

That discovery begins with a conscious decision to make some new choices.

God honors that commitment and attitude. Notice how He acknowledged Daniel's commitment:

> *Since the first day that you set your mind to gain understanding and to humble yourself before your God, your words were heard, and I have come in response to them.*
>
> Daniel 10:12

Jesus even said that we must make carefully thought-out decisions:

> *Love the Lord your God with all your heart and with all your soul and with all your mind.*
>
> Matthew 22:37

How do you make those mental choices, those choices that may include the heart and emotions but are nevertheless conscious, thought-out decisions?

Well, first it is important to understand that if God can be trusted, He can be trusted to help you make the right decisions, and you can have confidence in that.

Isaiah spoke to that very confidence.

> *You will keep in perfect peace him whose mind is steadfast, because he trusts in you. Trust in the LORD forever, for the LORD, the LORD, is the Rock eternal.*
>
> Isaiah 26:3–4

When we're trusting and dependent on God's protection and direction, He will not let us down. In fact, He gives us a very powerful promise:

> *Trust in the LORD with all your heart and lean not on your own understanding; in all your ways acknowledge him, and he will direct your paths.*
>
> Proverbs 3:5–6

What an amazing promise for protection. God promises that if you will trust in Him, depend on Him, not make your decisions with your own logic and understanding, *and* acknowledge that He is who He is – your King and Lord – He will lead you to the right choices and decisions.

David, the psalmist, understood that and asked God to make sure his mind was right with Him. He knew how important that is.

> *Test me, O LORD, and try me, examine my heart and my mind.*
>
> Psalm 26:2

How can you get to the point where you can make those right decisions and choices? By renewing or rebuilding your mind according to God's plans. That's what the apostle Paul was teaching at the beginning of Romans 12.

> *Therefore, I urge you, brothers, in view of God's mercy, to offer your*

> *bodies as living sacrifices, holy and*
> *pleasing to God—this is your spiri-*
> *tual act of worship. Do not conform*
> *any longer to the pattern of this*
> *world, but be transformed by the re-*
> *newing of your mind. Then you will*
> *be able to test and approve what*
> *God's will is—his good, pleasing*
> *and perfect will.*
>
> Romans 12:1–2

See how important a renewed mind is? With a renewed mind you will be able to determine and confirm God's will for you!

Using that passage from Romans, let's take a look at how you can get a renewed mind.

Come Before God as a Living Sacrifice

This is curious. Generally the purpose of a sacrifice is to pay the price for sin. However, the Bible says that Jesus was the sacrifice for our sin.

> *...Christ would have had to suffer*
> *many times since the creation of the*
> *world. But now he has appeared once*
> *for all at the end of the ages to do away*
> *with sin by the sacrifice of himself.*
>
> Hebrews 9:26

So what does a living sacrifice do? In order to grasp that, we need to understand the concept of a sacrifice.

First of all, a sacrifice has a purpose.

Many different kinds of sacrifices were required and offered in the Old Testament. They varied from sacrifices for sin to sacrifices for fellowship. Each sacrifice had its own purpose.

Likewise, if you are going to be a living sacrifice, you must realize that you have a purpose – that God has a purpose for your life. As God is committed to that purpose for your life, so you must be committed to it.

When your dreams have been broken into pieces, it's hard to believe that life can ever be good or right again. But hold onto this key thought: your life is not defined by your loss or failure, or even by your circumstances. Your life is defined by God's purpose for you.

In my personal Bible study, one of my favorite things has been to study the lives of those whose names were changed by God, men such as Abraham, Jacob, and Paul. In each case, when God changed their name, He gave them a new name that defined their ministry.

That's what they were known for. Not their failures and sinfulness, but their ministry – their purpose.

Your life is not defined by your loss or failure, or even by your circumstances. Your life is defined by God's purpose for you.

As a living sacrifice, you are defined by your purpose.

Secondly, a sacrifice was to be totally consumed.

You don't read about half-burnt sacrifices in the Bible. Sacrifices were totally burned up or cooked or poured out. There were no partial sacrifices.

As a living sacrifice, you also must be totally consumed – totally devoted or immersed in obedience and commitment to God's leading.

Thirdly, a sacrifice was offered according to specific instructions.

Read the eighth chapter of Leviticus and catch how detailed the instructions were for the sacrifices. The instructions weren't meant to be tedious. It's just that each meticulous requirement had meaning and purpose.

The same thing is true for us regarding our call to be living sacrifices. We have specific directives, and we are to live out our lives according to the instruction of the Word of God.

Our instructions have meaning and purpose. Don't fail to follow God's leading in His Word.

Fourthly, a sacrifice totally submits. In other words, the sacrifice yielded its own will.

This is so very important to understand. Sometimes we make a grave error in our commitment to God by controlling our commitment. In other words, we maintain our will over God's will even though we have chosen to obey Him.

We control our obedience. We control our devotion. We control our submission.

Sacrificial submission gives up control. It is exactly what Jesus did in the Garden of Gethsemane before His crucifixion when He asked the Father for an option, but yielded and said, *"...not my will, but yours be done"* (Luke 22:42).

We sometimes use the term "dying to self" to describe this submission. It is a realization and commitment that your life belongs to God—completely. You no longer control your life. He does.

> *Through Jesus, therefore, let us continually offer to God a sacrifice of praise—the fruit of lips that confess his name.*
>
> Hebrews 13:15

Come Before God as Holy

The second thing the apostle Paul teaches us in Romans 12 about renewing our mind is that we are to be holy. This is such a foreign concept for most people, even many Christians. However, as a believer and follower of God you are called to be holy. You may not act like it, but you are called to be holy.

But just as he who called you is holy,
so be holy in all you do; for it is writ-
ten: "Be holy, because I am holy."
                              1 Peter 1:15–16

The word "holy" means set apart, consecrated for God's purpose. It's not an action or an attitude, it's a position and a commitment.

To be holy means you understand that God has called you to a special kind of devotion. Your life is not your own, it is God's, and He can do whatever He chooses with you and through you.

This is why so many Christians live unfulfilled lives. They are resisting the fact that God has consecrated them for His purpose. They find themselves in a spiritual limbo where they don't belong to the world, but they aren't in a position to be used or blessed by God.

If you are resisting living out God's purpose and will for your life, you are miserable.

There is a tremendous sense of awe and wonder when we come into the presence of God, realizing that we are "called," "set apart," and "consecrated" for His purposes.

...we have been made holy through
the sacrifice of the body of Jesus
Christ once for all.
                              Hebrews 10:10

When you understand that call to holiness, you go into the world with an overwhelming sense of responsibility. Suddenly you realize that you can't live out your responsibility on your own. You realize that you NEED God. You realize that you can't do this in your own strength. You need supernatural power.

But there's more to renewing your mind.

Come Before God as Pleasing

This became one of the most life-changing yet practical discoveries in my life: I am to please God!

> *As you come to him, the living Stone—rejected by men but chosen by God and precious to him—you also, like living stones, are being built into a spiritual house to be a holy priesthood, offering spiritual sacrifices acceptable to God through Jesus Christ.*
>
> 1 Peter 2:4–5

The word used here for "acceptable" is essentially the same as the word "pleasing" in Romans 12:1–2. However, in either case, it doesn't mean that we have to try to impress God. I daresay none of us has impressed God. Not that He isn't overwhelmingly in love with us, but He knows us so well that we're not going to surprise Him.

What is pleasing and fully acceptable to God? The Bible lists a number of things that please God, and we would do well to learn these things:

God is pleased when we live empowered by the Holy Spirit.

> *For the kingdom of God is not a matter of eating and drinking, but of righteousness, peace and joy in the Holy Spirit, because anyone who serves Christ in this way is pleasing to God and approved by men.*
>
> Romans 14:17–18

I know this sounds weird, but God is pleased when we suffer for being godly.

> *...But if you suffer for doing good and you endure it, this is pleasing before God.*
>
> 1 Peter 2:20

It pleases God when you take care of your family.

> *But if a widow has children or grand-children, these should learn first of*

> *all to put their religion into practice*
> *by caring for their own family and*
> *so repaying their parents and grand-*
> *parents, for this is pleasing to God.*
>
> 1 Timothy 5:4

God is pleased with prayer.

> *I urge, then, first of all, that requests,*
> *prayers, intercession and thanksgiv-*
> *ing be made for everyone—for kings*
> *and all those in authority, that we*
> *may live peaceful and quiet lives in*
> *all godliness and holiness. This is*
> *good, and pleases God our Savior…*
>
> 1 Timothy 2:1–3

So, as we are directed in Romans 12:1 to be holy and pleasing to God, obedience to that leads to what we're taught in verse 2 – to develop a new mindset, one that God wants us to have.

Romans 12:2 basically says: *Don't conform. Transform!*

Let's look at how that happens.

Don't Conform

"Do not conform" basically means *"Don't be motivated by this day and age, or let this time that*

you're living in dictate and control your life."

The apostle Paul drew a very disturbing picture of what happens when God's people conform.

> *Now these things occurred as examples to keep us from setting our hearts on evil things as they did. Do not be idolaters, as some of them were; as it is written: "The people sat down to eat and drink and got up to indulge in pagan revelry." We should not commit sexual immorality, as some of them did—and in one day twenty-three thousand of them died. We should not test the Lord, as some of them did—and were killed by snakes. And do not grumble, as some of them did—and were killed by the destroying angel. These things happened to them as examples and were written down as warnings for us, on whom the fulfillment of the ages has come.*
>
> 1 Corinthians 10:6–11

To conform means to settle for less than God's purpose and plan. Many Christians damage themselves spiritually, as well as other ways, when they compromise and water down God's intent for their lives.

I've seen so many Christians who for some reason thought it was a good idea to combine biblical
truth with worldly philosophies including horo-
scopes, fortunetelling, other religions, or worldly
logic. That is just plain dangerous.

It makes no sense whatsoever to take the truth
and teaching of the Creator and Sustainer of Life
and try to improve on it by combining it with the
misguided principles, deceit, and lies of anyone
or anything else.

> *See to it that no one takes you captive*
> *through hollow and deceptive phi-*
> *losophy, which depends on human*
> *tradition and the basic principles of*
> *this world rather than on Christ.*
>
> Colossians 2:8

To conform is also to be motivated by sin.

> *Do not love the world or anything in*
> *the world. If anyone loves the world,*
> *the love of the Father is not in him.*
> *For everything in the world—the*
> *cravings of sinful man, the lust of*
> *his eyes and the boasting of what he*
> *has and does—comes not from the*
> *Father but from the world.*
>
> 1 John 2:15–16

What motivates you? Was it improper motivation that got you to where you are right now? If so, get that settled with God and find your motivation in Him.

You see, we're motivated by whatever we set our sights on. What or who are you paying attention to? That's what will influence your life.

The apostle Paul warned about that:

> *Since you died with Christ to the basic principles of this world, why, as though you still belonged to it, do you submit to its rules: "Do not handle! Do not taste! Do not touch!"? These are all destined to perish with use, because they are based on human commands and teachings. Such regulations indeed have an appearance of wisdom, with their self-imposed worship, their false humility and their harsh treatment of the body, but they lack any value in restraining sensual indulgence. Since, then, you have been raised with Christ, set your hearts on things above, where Christ is seated at the right hand of God. Set your minds on things above, not on earthly things.*
>
> Colossians 2:20 – 3:2

We're motivated by whatever we set our sights on.

What have you been focusing on lately? What philosophy or life principles have you been following? Are they godly truths and principles or a combination of other thoughts and philosophies?

Just because someone says their way works doesn't mean it is right. How does it compare to what God says? Be careful not to be deceived by those who take biblical truths and twist them out of context – those teachings and philosophies that Colossians refers to as *"the appearance of wisdom."*

Rather, set your sights on God's ways.

Be Transformed

This could be one of those life changing moments for you.

We generally think that if our life needs a change then it is up to us to make it happen. However, that is wrong thinking. Notice that the verse doesn't say "transform yourself."

So how do you get transformed?

It's something that God does. God is in the business of transforming your life.

If you've been trying to transform your own life you are one frustrated person.

The problem is that when we try to transform our own life, we just create more problems because we have a sinful nature. That nature leads to more sin.

But when God transforms our lives, it leads to truth and wholeness and victory in life.

How does He do it? He begins by establishing His relationship with you, by coming into your life to develop you into what His plans have been for you all along.

As He reveals Himself to you, and you get to know Him, your way of thinking changes.

> *...put on the new self, which is being renewed in knowledge in the image of its Creator.*
>
> Colossians 3:10

And He begins to give you a whole new mind-set, a whole new understanding.

> *Be renewed in the spirit of your mind...*
>
> Ephesians 4:23

God begins to refocus you on Him. He does it by renewing your life through His Holy Spirit.

> *He saved us, not because of righteous things we had done, but because of His mercy. He saved us through the*

washing of rebirth and renewal by the Holy Spirit, whom He poured out on us generously through Jesus Christ our Savior.

Titus 3:5–6

Dear God,
I need a fresh outlook on life. I need to think differently about things. I've let my circumstances control my thinking, and I am ready to see things from a different perspective. God, I'm submitting myself to You as a living sacrifice. I know You have a purpose and plan, and I want to be a part of that. So I give myself to You and ask that You renew my mind. Change my way of thinking. Help me to see things through You.

Amen

Principle #3
Probabilities Versus
Possibilities

Coming to grips with a new future can be daunting, but it should begin with looking at the possibilities and opportunities. If you can't see at least some of the possibilities or opportunities that God might open up for you, you need to spend some time on this principle.

Most of us make plans for the future based on our past. We forget that the future is uncharted territory. If we plan for it according to our past and present, that's pretty much all we'll have in the future.

What are God's possibilities in your life? When God looks at you, what kind of potential does He see? Where does God want to take you? Just how big are God's plans for your life?

For nothing is impossible with God.
Luke 1:37

That verse is huge! If we don't really believe it then we can't possibly be ready to accept it as truth with all its implications in our personal life.

If we don't really believe that in our life everything is possible with God, it affects the way we live. We get discouraged and in bondage.

> *Then the LORD said to Moses, "Now you will see what I will do to Pharaoh: Because of my mighty hand he will let them go; because of my mighty hand he will drive them out of his country." Moses reported this to the Israelites, but they did not listen to him because of their discouragement and cruel bondage.*
>
> Exodus 6:1,9

It amazes me that some people accept a lifestyle of discouragement and bondage. They just seem to give up and assume that is how it will be for the rest of their life.

Why would you succumb to that? For the same reason the Israelites did. They couldn't see beyond the realities of their lives.

It is such a contrast to what Jesus said:

> *Then you will know the truth, and the truth will set you free. So if the*

> *Son sets you free, you will be free in-*
> *deed.*
>
> John 8:32,36

Paul explained it this way:

> *I know what it is to be in need, and I*
> *know what it is to have plenty. I have*
> *learned the secret of being content*
> *in any and every situation, whether*
> *well fed or hungry, whether living in*
> *plenty or in want. I can do everything*
> *through him who gives me strength.*
>
> Philippians 4:12–13

What Paul was saying was that the circumstances of his life didn't define him. He was defined by what God did through him.

If we are focused on our circumstances and past experience, we have a very limited and self-centered viewpoint in life.

We Want Our Way

Notice this characteristic in the Israelites in the desert.

> *In the desert the whole community*
> *grumbled against Moses and Aaron.*

The Israelites said to them, "If only we had died by the Lord's hand in Egypt! There we sat around pots of meat and ate all the food we wanted, but you have brought us out into this desert to starve this entire assembly to death." Then the LORD said to Moses, "I will rain down bread from heaven for you. The people are to go out each day and gather enough for that day. In this way I will test them and see whether they will follow my instructions."

Exodus 16: 2–4

This is so important to understand.

God had not forgotten about the Israelites in the desert! It wasn't as though He got busy or distracted and the great exodus slipped His mind.

No, instead of truly seeking God's direction and presence, all the people could think about was their situation. And their circumstances were more important to them than what God was up to.

They missed out on what God wanted to teach them: to be obedient and sensitive to His leading.

Why was that important? Because God really did have their best interests at heart. He knew what was ahead and how important it was for them to be committed to following and obeying Him.

We're Afraid

Even people who saw Jesus do miraculous works were skeptical and afraid. They were afraid of how He would affect their lifestyle. They were afraid of what the authorities might do. They might even have been afraid of what He would do.

> *And the people went out to see what had happened. When they came to Jesus, they found the man from whom the demons had gone out, sitting at Jesus' feet, dressed and in his right mind; and they were afraid. Those who had seen it told the people how the demon-possessed man had been cured. Then all the people of the region of the Gerasenes asked Jesus to leave them, because they were overcome with fear. So he got into the boat and left.*
>
> Luke 8:35–37

Most people have a learned pessimism. They have gotten so discouraged and beat down in life that they're afraid to think beyond that reality. In fact, they may think it is irresponsible to think otherwise.

Above All, We Think In Probabilities

Just as the people who were afraid of Jesus asked Him to leave, we essentially do the same when we fail to see that God is up to something in our lives. That happens because we base our thinking on the things that have gone wrong in our life. We think that because certain things have not gone well, we can expect more of the same.

In a sense, we're right. If we continue living and thinking the same way, we have no right to think things will change. That's what probability thinking does.

When we live anticipating probabilities, we don't open ourselves up to the truth that nothing is impossible with God. For most people, the idea that "all things are possible with God" is not really a belief, it's a wish.

The truth is that most of us think in probabilities. We look at our circumstances, and we plan for what we consider to be the most probable thing that will happen. We define God by our circumstances and the probabilities of what we think will happen.

But God thinks in possibilities.

We define God by our circumstances and the probabilities of what we think will happen.
But God thinks in possibilities.
He is not limited by your circumstances.

He is not limited by your circumstances. As we've already seen, Sarah's barren state didn't prevent God from fulfilling His plan to give Abraham a son.

Earlier we looked at the exodus of the Israelites across the desert. The escape started with some very dire circumstances. In fact, at one point they were cornered between the sea and the Egyptian army that was chasing them down.

> *The Egyptians—all Pharaoh's horses and chariots, horsemen and troops—pursued the Israelites and overtook them as they camped by the sea near Pi Hahiroth, opposite Baal Zephon. As Pharaoh approached, the Israelites looked up, and there were the Egyptians, marching after them. They were terrified and cried out to the LORD.*
>
> *Then Moses stretched out his hand over the sea, and all that night the LORD drove the sea back with a strong east wind and turned it into dry land. The waters were divided, and the Israelites went through the sea on dry ground, with a wall of water on their right and on their left.*
>
> Exodus 14:9–10,21–22

Now, if God can cause a ninety-year-old woman to get pregnant, and He can open the sea as an escape route for the fleeing Hebrews, don't you think He can overcome the circumstances in your life to accomplish His plan?

Even if you have trouble believing God can do something that incredible for you, it doesn't limit God.

It didn't matter that Sarah didn't or couldn't believe. God said it would happen, and He even put it on the calendar! Nor did it matter that the Israelites feared for their lives. God knew what He was up to!

God may choose not to respond because of one's lack of faith, but He's not limited by it.

> *Coming to his hometown, he began teaching the people in their synagogue, and they were amazed. "Where did this man get this wisdom and these miraculous powers?" they asked. "Isn't this the carpenter's son? Isn't his mother's name Mary, and aren't his brothers James, Joseph, Simon and Judas? Aren't all his sisters with us? Where then did this man get all these things?" And they took offense at him. But Jesus said to them, "Only in his hometown*

*and in his own house is a prophet
without honor." And he did not do
many miracles there because of their
lack of faith.*

Matthew 13:54–58

On the other hand, note the encounter Jesus had
with a father who asked Jesus to heal his son who
had severe seizures. The father asked Jesus, *"…if
you can do anything, take pity on us and help us."*
Look at what followed:

*"'If you can'?" said Jesus. "Every-
thing is possible for him who believes." Immediately the boy's father
exclaimed, "I do believe; help me
overcome my unbelief!"*

Mark 9:23–24

And Jesus healed him. He wasn't limited by
the father's unbelief.

*What if some did not have faith?
Will their lack of faith nullify God's
faithfulness? Not at all…!*

Romans 3:3–4a

Nor is God limited by the requirements of your
circumstances. Again, referring back to Abraham

and Sarah's desire to get pregnant, Sarah was too old. Even Abraham wondered if he wasn't too old.

> *Abraham fell facedown; he laughed and said to himself, "Will a son be born to a man a hundred years old? Will Sarah bear a child at the age of ninety?"*

> Genesis 17:17

What kind of requirements do your needs demand? God is not limited by those requirements.

Psalm 78 records some incidents in the desert when the Israelites were on their way to the Promised Land. They were out of water — there was no water in the desert. Water requires a source. They were out of grain — you can't grow wheat in the desert. It requires crops and water and fertile soil. They had no meat — you can't raise animals in the desert. It requires water and grain.

But those requirements didn't stop God.

> *They spoke against God, saying, "Can God spread a table in the desert? When he struck the rock, water gushed out, and streams flowed abundantly. But can he also give us food? Can he supply meat for his*

> *people?" ...For they did not believe*
> *in God or trust in his deliverance.*
> Psalm 78:19–20,22

God doesn't think in probabilities. I doubt He
has ever even used the word "probably." God
looks at the impossibilities and considers them
possibilities.

That's exactly how God thinks about you. He's
not limited by the probabilities or the impossibilities, and He doesn't want you to think that
way either.

Look at how Paul explained possibility thinking:

> *His intent was that now, through*
> *the church, the manifold wisdom of*
> *God should be made known to the*
> *rulers and authorities in the heav-*
> *enly realms, according to his eternal*
> *purpose which he accomplished in*
> *Christ Jesus our Lord. In him and*
> *through faith in him we may ap-*
> *proach God with freedom and con-*
> *fidence. I ask you, therefore, not to*
> *be discouraged because of my suffer-*
> *ings for you, which are your glory.*
> *For this reason I kneel before the*
> *Father, from whom his whole fam-*

ily in heaven and on earth derives its name. I pray that out of his glorious riches he may strengthen you with power through his Spirit in your inner being, so that Christ may dwell in your hearts through faith. And I pray that you, being rooted and established in love, may have power, together with all the saints, to grasp how wide and long and high and deep is the love of Christ, and to know this love that surpasses knowledge—that you may be filled to the measure of all the fullness of God.

Ephesians 3:10–19

Now, don't get possibility thinking confused with positive thinking.

Probability thinking dwells on the present and is rooted in the past. Positive thinking is an attitude that focuses on the things you want to happen. Possibility thinking is focused on what God wants to do.

God's possibilities aren't dependent on man's probabilities.

Joseph had lost everything. You can read about it starting in Genesis 37. He had been wronged every way possible. His own brothers sold him into slavery. He was separated from his home-land and family. His owner falsely accused him of attempting to rape his wife. He was sent to prison for something he didn't do, and then for-gotten. The probability was that he would die there.

But he continued to trust God.

And God began to open doors. It wasn't long before Joseph was put in charge of the prison – a prisoner in charge of the prison! Only God could work out something like that. Eventually the Pharaoh discovered Joseph's worth and put him to work.

Under God's providence, Joseph was placed in the position of what we would call the prime min-ister.

As has happened many times in history, when the countries around Egypt were suffering severe drought, Egypt had food – mostly because of the fertile lands around the Nile River.

Joseph's brothers came looking for food, hav-ing no idea what had happened to Joseph. He recognized them, but they had no clue as to who he was. He provided food and supplies for them. Eventually the truth came out and Joseph made an amazing statement:

> *But Joseph said to them, "Don't be*
> *afraid. Am I in the place of God?*

You intended to harm me, but God intended it for good to accomplish what is now being done, the saving of many lives."

Genesis 50:19–20

That must have rocked their world!

Notice four things that you need to remember about God's possibilities in your time of difficulty.

First of all, don't panic.

God is in control. While the circumstances may not seem like it at times, God has never been controlled by circumstances. Never.

Secondly, ask yourself the question Joseph asked: "Am I in the place of God?" In other words, "Am I in God's will?"

Be very careful not to answer that based on your circumstances. Circumstances can change and be changed. They are not a fair guideline to determine God's will and thinking. After all, Joseph had horrible circumstances, but he was right where God could use him.

However, if you know you are not in God's will, then you obviously need to make that right with God.

Thirdly, even when you suffer the consequences of your own sin or someone else's sin, God can use that to put you in a place where He can use you.

If God did that with Joseph, He can certainly do that with you!

Fourthly, never underestimate what God can accomplish by what you are going through right now.

With that in mind, what might God want to do in and through your life? Where does God want to take you? What might He want to accomplish through your life?

It's time to start dreaming about the possibilities in your future.

You see, possibilities are about the future. When your life has been shattered it's difficult to think about the possible future, but just because the past or the present is negative doesn't mean the future must be.

> *But as for me, I will always have hope; I will praise you more and more.*
>
> *My mouth will tell of your righteousness, of your salvation all day long, though I know not its measure.*
>
> *I will come and proclaim your mighty acts, O Sovereign LORD; I will proclaim your righteousness, yours alone.*
>
> *Since my youth, O God, you have taught me, and to this day I declare your marvelous deeds.*

Even when I am old and gray, do not forsake me, O God, till I declare your power to the next generation, your might to all who are to come.

Your righteousness reaches to the skies, O God, you who have done great things.

Who, O God, is like you?

Though you have made me see troubles, many and bitter, you will restore my life again; from the depths of the earth you will again bring me up.

You will increase my honor and comfort me once again.

I will praise you with the harp for your faithfulness, O my God; I will sing praise to you with the lyre, O Holy One of Israel.

My lips will shout for joy when I sing praise to you—I, whom you have redeemed.

My tongue will tell of your righteous acts all day long, for those who wanted to harm me have been put to shame and confusion.

Psalm 71:14–24

The only thing that got Jesus through that horrible experience on the cross was the future.

Things couldn't have been worse. Death would be an escape from what Jesus was going through. He was in so much pain, so much sorrow, so much depression that He wondered why God had abandoned Him.

> *About the ninth hour Jesus cried out in a loud voice, "Eloi, Eloi, lama sabachthani?"—which means, "My God, my God, why have you forsaken me?"*
>
> Matthew 27:46

It was devastating. This Man who had healed so many, who had given hope to so many, who never hurt anyone, was dying from the worst form of capital punishment the world has ever known, for something He didn't do. It wasn't fair. It wasn't right. He was a good Man who lived a good life destroyed by an ignorant and cruel people.

But even at the end of His life, Jesus began to think of the future. His very last words before He died are a clarion call for hope.

> *Jesus called out with a loud voice, "Father, into your hands I commit my spirit." When he had said this, he breathed his last.*
>
> Luke 23:46

Even at the worst moment of His life, Jesus knew there was a future and He committed Himself to it. Talk about possibility thinking!

Now, if Jesus could think of the future at a time like that, surely we must also seek the future at the broken point of our life.

I love how David looked to the future at one of the lowest points of his life:

> *Create in me a pure heart, O God, and renew a steadfast spirit within me.*
>
> *Do not cast me from your presence or take your Holy Spirit from me.*
>
> *Restore to me the joy of your salvation and grant me a willing spirit, to sustain me.*
>
> *Then I will teach transgressors your ways, and sinners will turn back to you.*
>
> *Save me from bloodguilt, O God, the God who saves me, and my tongue will sing of your righteousness.*
>
> *O Lord, open my lips, and my mouth will declare your praise.*
>
> Psalm 51:10–15

David began to focus on his future by settling his past and taking the right steps in the present.

Interestingly, the first three things he determined that needed to happen were things that only God could do. This is something you need in your life right now.

First of all, he asked God for renewal. That meant taking away the unclean part of his past and "renewing" a steadfast spirit in him.

The Hebrew word for "renew" means to rebuild or repair. And the word for "spirit" is the same word for breath. That is exactly what God wants to do in your life. He wants to repair you. He wants to help you breathe again!

Secondly, he understood how important it was to stay in God's presence. He desperately needed God in his life, and so he asked God to keep him within His presence.

It is important to note that the presence of God involves many things: fellowship, submission to His will, worship, and even protection and provision from God.

Thirdly, he asked God for renewed joy.

Joy is an amazing element of a right relationship with God. The word doesn't necessarily mean happiness, although that certainly may be something you sense. It actually means "brightness." In other words, a sense that the darkness is lifting and that light is coming back into your life.

As I write this book, my father has been going through some very difficult times with his health. The long hard years on the mission field have taken their toll. Recently we were chatting about nothing in particular. I asked him how he was holding up. He said, "I still have light."

That is what joy is all about. It's not about being happy. David wasn't asking for happiness. He was asking for the dawn to break in his life.

Joy is about coming out of the darkness and seeing life from a new perspective.

David understood that his response to God's work in his life would produce three things.

- He would have a new testimony.

David had blown his testimony. Here he was the king, called by God, and anointed to this most important role. God had saved him from death many times. He had been used mightily by the Lord to exalt the name of God, and even after all that he had failed Him.

But David understood that God could restore his testimony – his ministry.

- He knew God's righteousness would overcome his guilt.

Think of righteousness as a three-dimensional word meaning clean, just, and right. But it is far more than that. It has a causative effect. In other words, because God is righteous, He causes righteousness.

This is so important to understand. Whether you're guilty of doubting God or committing some horrendous act, God's righteousness and forgiveness are bigger than your sin, your weakness, or your failure. Because God is righteous, He causes you to become clean, just, and right.

- He was aware that when God moved in his life, his worship would never be the same!

David's statement is quite astounding. He basically said, "Lord, if You will free me from this burden, I will praise You."

He wasn't making a deal with God. He understood that he was going through a process, and that at some point he would be ready, willing, and able to proclaim the praises of God.

Think about that. God is ready to move you from where you are right now to where you can, as David did, proclaim His praises. Not for His ego, but to change the world!

So think of the possibilities. What has to happen in your life for you to get to the point where you openly acknowledge God's greatness in your life?

Once you can answer that question, watch what God does!

What has to happen in your life for you to get to the point where you openly acknowledge God's greatness in your life?

Job, having lost everything in his life, understood this magnificent truth:

> *God is exalted in his power. Who is a teacher like him?*
> *Who has prescribed his ways for him, or said to him, "You have done wrong"?*
> *Remember to extol his work, which men have praised in song.*
> *All mankind has seen it; men gaze on it from afar.*
> *How great is God—beyond our understanding!*
>
> Job 36:22–26

Dear God,
All I've been able to think about is the past and the present. But I need a future, and I need a future with You. God, I don't know how You can get me from where I am to where You want me to be, but I'm willing to let You. So help me to see the possibilities, to think about where You want me and what You want to do. And, God, if there is anything I need right now, it's joy – a little brightness in my life.

Amen

Principle #4
Take Small Steps

One of the big mistakes we make when we are in a crisis situation is that we try to get as far away as we can from the problem. We tend to take giant strides to move beyond the crisis as quickly as possible, sometimes in any direction just to get away. But the key to successfully moving beyond the crisis is to move along the path that God wants you to take.

David sang a great song of worship to the Lord regarding his deliverance from his enemies. In that song he sang:

> *You broaden the path beneath me,*
> *so that my ankles do not turn.*
>
> 2 Samuel 22:37

What he was saying was that as he followed God's path away from the crisis, God made the path easier. The implication is that the path is not particularly easy at first.

Now, sometimes the crisis demands immediate flight, especially when one's life is in danger. However, sometimes getting away from the crisis requires a different approach, especially if the path is difficult and dangerous.

If your life is shattered because of a financial crisis, the death of a loved one, a divorce, or any number of other devastating experiences, your next step is a critical one. And so is the next one, and the next one.

In those cases, running or moving quickly in any direction just to get away can be treacherous.

It is usually far more beneficial in the long run to start off with deliberate, careful small steps in the right direction. Small steps in the right direction do a couple of important things for us.

First of all, while they move us away from the crisis, we build trust in God and a renewal of a healthy self-confidence.

This is important to understand. Self-confidence without trust in God is arrogance. As our trust in God grows, we begin to understand how much He cares for us. That in turn affirms our worth in Him, and that is a healthy self-confidence.

Secondly, as we move away from the difficult situation by taking small, careful steps, we focus on something else. We focus on the right direction. We concentrate on doing the right things. Eventually we have a new goal and a renewed sense of destiny.

How can you make sure you are taking the right steps in the right direction? Let's look at some scriptural instruction on six steps that God says you should take.

- **Seek to please God.**

  If the LORD delights in a man's way, he makes his steps firm; though he stumble, he will not fall, for the LORD upholds him with his hand.
  Psalm 37:23–24

This is the foundation. Choose to live in such a way that God will be delighted with you. When you are seeking to please God, God promises to steady you.

- **Memorize scripture.**

  The law of his God is in his heart; his feet do not slip.
  Psalm 37:31

To use a computer analogy, we are programmed or we program ourselves to act and react to certain situations. For example, a child will scream and throw a tantrum when they don't get their way until they have learned not to do that, until they have been programmed to respond differently.

When I was a teenager I thought it was cool to smoke. I had programmed myself to think that way. I soon discovered that when I was stressed or troubled I needed a cigarette. It wasn't until I realized how uncool it really is that I changed that behavior and programmed myself not to smoke.

When you program your life with the Word of God that is how you will respond and react when the pressure is on.

Find Scripture that speaks to your needs and memorize it. Even if it's just a verse a week, start reprogramming your mind.

We saw this in Principle 2 – Rebuild Your Mind.

> *Do not conform any longer to the pattern of this world, but be transformed by the renewing of your mind. Then you will be able to test and approve what God's will is—His good, pleasing and perfect will.*
>
> Romans 12:2

- **Follow biblical principles.**

Direct my footsteps according to your word; let no sin rule over me.

Psalm 119:133

You need to let God use His Word to direct your path. He created life. His life principles are solid, and He expects you to follow them.

I have a friend who was dealing with a terrible financial mess in his life. He is a Christian and really seeks to obey God. He's a great husband and father and is active in his church. But his finances were a mess.

I had never gotten into a discussion with him about money, but one day we were having coffee and he opened up about this issue in his life.

It soon became apparent that his whole financial structure was based on some principles he had learned from a book written by a money guru. And, frankly, most of the principles were contrary to biblical principles.

I asked him why he didn't follow the biblical principles for his finances.

His answer was, "Oh, you mean tithing? I've tried that. It doesn't work."

Clearly, he knew almost nothing of the sound biblical principles related to finances. And there are lots of them!

I asked him if he knew that well over a hundred verses in the Bible mention money and only a handful mention the tithe.

There are verses that talk about saving, borrowing, planning, investing, budgeting, negotiating, and yes even spending.

If you are determined to live within God's will, you must also live by His principles. And all the life principles you need are right there in His Word. To fail to follow them is sin, which just makes the problem worse.

> *His divine power has given us everything we need for life and godliness through our knowledge of him who called us by his own glory and goodness.*
>
> 2 Peter 1:3

Spend time in God's Word, and get to know and apply the principles that you need.

- **Act with wisdom.**

> *I guide you in the way of wisdom and lead you along straight paths. When you walk, your steps will not be hampered; when you run, you will not stumble.*
>
> Proverbs 4:11–12

This step is a natural follow-up to following godly biblical principles.

Here's a good definition for wisdom: the applied knowledge of God.

The applied knowledge of God makes you sure-footed in life. Wisdom goes hand-in-hand with confidence because you know God and know His truths and principles work, and can be trusted.

When Israel was about to enter the land God had promised them, He gave them this directive about His laws and principles through Moses:

> *Observe them carefully, for this will show your wisdom and understanding to the nations, who will hear about all these decrees and say, "Surely this great nation is a wise and understanding people."*
>
> Deuteronomy 4:6

Now, when He said *"Observe them carefully,"* He was saying be careful to apply them the right way. It doesn't do you any good to know God's truths and not apply them. But to know them and apply them to your life not only changes you; it also affects those connected to you.

- **Make sure your plans line up with God's.**

Wisdom: the applied knowledge of God.

In his heart a man plans his course, but the LORD determines his steps.

Proverbs 16:9

I've always been amazed at the plans some people come up with to solve their problems!

I came across a guy who had gone through a gut-wrenching divorce. A few years after the divorce, he was hanging out in bars because he believed he would find a woman who had gone through a similar experience, and they would understand each other and have a great relationship.

When I asked him how many women he had met who fit the bill, he answered, "Most of 'em."

"Well, why aren't you married yet?"

"Are you kidding? Most of 'em are really messed up."

I paused and then asked, "They wouldn't be thinking the same thing about you, would they?"

He just shrugged.

When your plans don't line up with God's, you are destined for more heartache.

- **Let Christ be your example.**

  To this you were called, because Christ suffered for you, leaving you

an example, that you should follow
in his steps.

1 Peter 2:21

Don't compare your circumstances and situation with others. Everyone's experience is different. Trying to act the way someone else did in a similar situation will just take your eyes off God's leading.

Asaph the psalmist had an interesting warning about this very thing:

> *But as for me, my feet had almost*
> *slipped; I had nearly lost my foothold.*
>
> *For I envied the arrogant when I*
> *saw the prosperity of the wicked.*
>
> *They have no struggles; their bodies are healthy and strong.*
>
> *They are free from the burdens*
> *common to man; they are not plagued*
> *by human ills.*
>
> *Therefore pride is their necklace;*
> *they clothe themselves with violence.*
>
> *From their callous hearts comes*
> *iniquity ; the evil conceits of their*
> *minds know no limits.*
>
> *They scoff, and speak with malice;*
> *in their arrogance they threaten oppression.*

*Their mouths lay claim to heaven,
and their tongues take possession of
the earth.*

*Therefore their people turn to them
and drink up waters in abundance.*

*They say, "How can God know?
Does the Most High have knowledge?"*

*This is what the wicked are like—
always carefree, they increase in
wealth.*

Psalm 73:2–12

Asaph is warning against losing your footing by focusing on what is going on in someone else's life.

When we have difficulties, others' lives seem so much better, even the wicked. One of the warning signs that you're not centered on following God is when you catch yourself asking, "Does God know what's going on?" or "How come that person gets all the breaks?" or "How is this fair?" or even "Am I doing the right thing by following God?"

As you take small steps away from the crisis in your life, and toward the Lord, keep your eyes on Him and not on other people and their circumstances.

One of the frustrating things about our walk with God is that He very seldom lays out His plan for us in advance. Usually we have to take it one step at a time.

Why?

Because He wants us to focus on the next step. We want to see where He's taking us, but right now getting there is far more important.

Take the next step. In the right direction.

> *Dear God,*
> *I just haven't been able to get away from this issue. I mean, I've tried but I just can't leave it behind. Would You help me to take the right steps in the right direction to get on with my life? God, if You'll show me the way, I'll follow. Help me to take these six steps, keep my eyes on You, and keep moving in the direction You want for my life.*
>
> *Amen*

Principle #5
How Much Are You Worth?

I've had the privilege of leading a number of Success Strategy Seminars through the years. These are seminars that help businesses create a more productive, efficient atmosphere and attitude in the workplace. The premise is that if your employees are personally successful, their attitude and focus will contribute to the success of your company.

One of the first things I ask the employees is "How much are you worth?" The response is always somewhat awkward. People immediately think of the answer in terms of money. But that's not the question. The question is "How much are *you* worth?" In other words, what is the value of your life? What is *your life* worth?

After a few moments of awkwardness I follow up with this statement: "Whatever you think you are worth in life, that's what you'll spend."

Then in a meeting with the management of the company I'll ask, "What are your employees worth?" And we go through the same awkward moments until I follow up with the statement, "Whatever you think your employees are worth, that's what they will spend."

So I ask you the question, "What are you worth?"

Whatever you think you are worth, that's what you will spend in life. If you don't think you are worth much, that's all you will spend. If you think your life is worth much, that's what you will spend.

Let me follow this line of thought up with another question: How much does God think you are worth?

This is one of the hardest things for us to understand. God has a premium on your life.

One of David's psalms addresses this very issue with some brilliant insight.

> *O LORD, you have searched me and you know me.*
>
> *You know when I sit and when I rise; you perceive my thoughts from afar.*
>
> *You discern my going out and my lying down; you are familiar with all my ways.*
>
> *Before a word is on my tongue you know it completely, O LORD.*

Whatever you think you are worth, that's what you will spend in life.

You hem me in—behind and before; you have laid your hand upon me.

Such knowledge is too wonderful for me, too lofty for me to attain.

Where can I go from your Spirit? Where can I flee from your presence?

If I go up to the heavens, you are there; if I make my bed in the depths, you are there.

If I rise on the wings of the dawn, if I settle on the far side of the sea, even there your hand will guide me, your right hand will hold me fast.

If I say, "Surely the darkness will hide me and the light become night around me," even the darkness will not be dark to you; the night will shine like the day, for darkness is as light to you.

For you created my inmost being; you knit me together in my mother's womb.

I praise you because I am fearfully and wonderfully made; your works are wonderful, I know that full well.

My frame was not hidden from you when I was made in the secret place. When I was woven together in the depths of the earth, your eyes saw my unformed body. All the days ordained for me were written in your book before one of them came to be.

How precious to me are your thoughts, O God! How vast is the sum of them!

Were I to count them, they would outnumber the grains of sand. When I awake, I am still with you.

Psalm 139:1 18

I wonder what was going through David's head when he wrote this. It probably took him some time to write it down exactly the way it needed to be said. What must he have been thinking about?

Well, if you look down toward the end of the psalm you get a glimpse of what was going on.

If only you would slay the wicked, O God! Away from me, you bloodthirsty men!

They speak of you with evil intent; your adversaries misuse your name.

Do I not hate those who hate you, O LORD, and abhor those who rise up against you?

I have nothing but hatred for them; I count them my enemies.
Psalm 139:19–22

From the time he was a little boy, David faced opposition and danger. His rise to authority was marked by grave challenges and threats. As a king, his life was constantly on the line. He must have had overwhelming stress to deal with.

In the midst of all that, David found great comfort and strength in remembering God's passion for His own creation. There were times when David looked around to see the handiwork of God and glory in it. But this time he looked at himself and realized something very special about God: we are of incredible worth to God.

I love how at the very beginning of this psalm, in the first verse, David makes such an overwhelming statement of grace. *"God, You know me inside and out. You know the good and the bad. Even the stuff I've tried to suppress, the things I've forgotten, the things I'm too ashamed to bring out, You know. You've been to the darkest corners of my life."*

With that statement, we are taken on a beautiful journey of realization.

God is so into you that He knows your every move – when you sit and when you walk. And He still loves you.

He completely understands your thoughts, even when you may not understand why you think the things you do. And He still loves you.

He knows when you get up in the morning and when you go to bed at night. He knows all about your ways and your habits, even the bad ones. And He still loves you.

Before you say something, even if you don't say something, God knows where it's coming from. And He still loves you.

He has surrounded you with Himself and, even more important, He has put His hand on you. You are chosen. You are called. You have a purpose and a destiny, because God still loves you.

That truth is so amazing to realize, yet too great to comprehend.

God, who loves you so much, will meet you anywhere you are, no matter if you are on the mountaintops of life or in the very depths of despair; no matter if you are soaring with eagles at the beginning of a new day—a new chapter of life— or have lost your way.

No matter where you find yourself, God is there to hold you and guide you, because He still loves you. And He won't let you go.

Even if you think it's so dark that God can't find you, and you'll never see the light of day again, know this: there is no darkness for God. And He still loves you.

Why?

Because He created you. He designed you. He planned you.

Think about it. Your body is such an intricate, awesome design. God did that!

You didn't just happen. You were made. Out of nothing, God made something special. You were a secret that God planned and held until just the right time. And He loves you.

You are so planned by God that He even planned your days before the first one happened.

He has so much invested in you and you are of such great worth to Him that He thinks about you all the time. God loves you so much!

> *How precious to me [about me] are your thoughts, O God! How vast is the sum of them!*
>
> *Were I to count them, they would outnumber the grains of sand...*
> Psalm 139:17–18

I put the brackets in that verse because that's what the Hebrew really means there. God thinks about you all the time!

If you are so well-planned, designed, and destined by God, doesn't it make sense that He has something pretty awesome in store for you at the end of this journey? Don't quit. Don't give up. Don't despair. You are worth far too much to God.

That's the apparent conclusion David came to at the end of the psalm.

> *Search me, O God, and know my heart; test me and know my anxious thoughts.*
>
> *See if there is any offensive way in me, and lead me in the way everlasting.*
>
> Psalm 139:23–24

David said, *"God, keep working in my life. Test me if You have to, but know that I'm anxious. And if there is something offensive in my life, lead me to the right way...the eternal way."*

That last phrase is a curious one. It's an affirmation that God is up to something eternal in your life.

What is happening in life here on earth is a preparation for eternal life!

We are, as we've already seen, eternal beings.

> *Now we know that if the earthly tent we live in is destroyed, we have a building from God, an eternal house in heaven, not built by human*

> *hands…For while we are in this tent,*
> *we groan and are burdened, because*
> *we do not wish to be unclothed but to*
> *be clothed with our heavenly dwell-*
> *ing, so that what is mortal may be*
> *swallowed up by life.*
>
> 2 Corinthians 5:1,4

Paul points out two very important things in this passage.

First, we are eternal beings, though currently in a temporal state. I love the way he describes it. We're living in tents. Not permanent buildings… yet. Tents. And I don't know about you, but my tent is getting a little worn.

Secondly, and this is so exciting, catch the last phrase in verse 4. When we die, we are *"swallowed up by life."* Did you get that? Not swallowed up by death, but by life!

This passage affirms that there are two phases of life: mortal life and immortal life…and death is the passing, the transition, the graduation from mortality to immortality – eternal life!

What is happening here on earth is part of God's eternal plan for you. You ain't seen nuthin' yet! I know that's not good grammar, but it's great theology!

So God has put a tremendous value on your life because He has eternal plans for you.

We are eternal beings,
though currently in a
temporal state.

That's why it was so important for Him to pay the penalty for your sin on the cross. If He hadn't done that, you would have no way to fulfill His eternal plans for your life! For that reason alone, you are worth that much to Him!

He was wanting and willing to pay whatever the price for you. And the final price was death.

Now, get this. When Jesus died on the cross He was saying, "You – YOU – are worth *more* than My death! I can make this investment in you because I know you're worth it!"

While we can only see the present and the past, God sees beyond all of that to the future, and He knows He made a good investment.

You may not feel worth it now, but God sees the end result. He knows what lies ahead. He knew it before He even created you. And He knows you're worth it!

So if you're worth that much...go spend yourself!

Dear God,
My life doesn't seem to have had much value lately. Not much of me to spend. God, I find it so hard to understand that I'm worth so much to You. But I really am grateful that You love me. I find it so amazing that I'm part of an eternal plan,

something that goes on beyond life here on earth. And if I'm that important to You, help me discover what You want to do in and through my life now.

Amen

Principle #6
Leave The Past

Some time ago my wife was involved in a bad car accident. An oncoming car lost control and veered into her lane, hitting her and rolling her car into a ditch. She was injured and the car was totaled. However, the police referred to it as a no-fault accident. Well, obviously someone was at fault, but the police chose not to attach blame.

Our society has attached the "no-fault" term to several "someone's-at-fault" situations. We have no-fault divorces, no-fault accidents, even no-fault insurance.

But get this: God offers "no-fault" recovery! This is one of the greatest principles you can ever discover.

God is offering you freedom from your past. Of course you're guilty of your sin. But God has even that covered. That's exactly why Jesus died on the cross – for your sin. You can't blame anyone else for Jesus' death. It was your fault. But

God says He's willing to free you from that fault if you will receive His forgiveness on His terms. And His terms are that He takes control of your life.

"Well, sure," you may say, "but what about the consequences and circumstances that dog me?"

I have a friend who was burned badly in a fire as a teenager. He still has a lot of scars from the incident.

One day we got to talking about the scars, and I asked how he felt about them.

He said, "My scars bother other people more than me. The way I look at it, the scars are proof that I survived. The scars tell me that I'm not on fire anymore."

Many of us have scar tissue from our past. Significant scar tissue. Sometimes it's scar tissue that is our fault. Sometimes it's scar tissue that is someone else's fault.

The problem so many of us have with the scars in our lives is that we can't get past them. We hate them. The guilt just seems to beat us down and overwhelm us. It's like our past is something that owns us, something we have to hold onto.

The only things worth holding onto in life are things of value. In a physical sense that would be such things as investments or antiques. In an emotional sense that would include memories. But when you hold onto the bad things, the difficult things, the things that were against you, you are saying they are worth something.

Now certainly there are some things we hold onto because we need closure, we seek justice, or for some reason beyond our control the matter has not been settled.

But I ask you: what is your past realistically worth today?

Paul must have dealt with a lot of regret since his job before he came to know the Lord was to persecute and even kill Christians. He explains how he dealt with his past this way:

> *Brothers, I do not consider myself yet to have taken hold of it. But one thing I do: Forgetting what is behind and straining toward what is ahead, I press on toward the goal to win the prize for which God has called me heavenward in Christ Jesus.*
>
> Philippians 3:13–14

It may be that you can't let go of the past. And that keeps you from moving past the issues and problems in life.

That's understandable. There are things in your past that are important to you: milestone events, life-altering occurrences. Memories... How do you get past that?

I knew an older man who was quite bitter. It seemed he had a sour attitude about everything.

His adult life was pretty normal. However, his youth had been extremely hard. He had been abandoned by his mother, and he grew up in an orphanage. When he got out of the orphanage he was on his own. He worked hard and tried to make a life for himself, but then the Great Depression set in and he lost everything, including his job. He almost starved to death.

It seemed that every time I spoke with him the conversation always turned to his past.

One day he made a curious statement. He said, "I love my past."

If your past was not a good thing, you're probably dealing with some of the consequences of it. If you let it continue to shape you, it will shape and mold you into more of what you are now.

If your past was a good thing, there is nothing wrong with holding onto those wonderful memories. You're not going to forget them, and you shouldn't.

But what's ahead?

Whether the past is a good memory or a bad memory, it is essentially used life. Used life!

In either case, it's time to reach for some fresh, unused life.

Therefore, since Christ suffered in his body, arm yourselves also with the same attitude, because he who has suffered in his body is done with sin. As a result, he does not live the rest of his earthly life for evil human desires, but rather for the will of God. For you have spent enough time in the past..

1 Peter 4:1–3

Did you get that? One who chooses to live in the will of God lets go of the past!

Why? Because God's will is not based on the past but on the future. It is God's intent for you to move on.

Forget the former things; do not dwell on the past.

Isaiah 43:18

I remember going to church youth camps as a teenager. More than once I heard a preacher say something like "How are you going to feel when you stand before God along with the rest of the world and a video gets played back of your life?"

I was horrified. I thought heaven is going to be pretty embarrassing. I mean, everyone will know for eternity what I've done, and they'll always think of that when they look at me.

As I grew older I realized that was just some shameless manipulation by some very misguided men. The truth is that God doesn't dwell on your past. He's all about your future.

> ...*For the past troubles will be forgotten and hidden from my eyes. Behold, I will create new heavens and a new earth. The former things will not be remembered, nor will they come to mind.*
>
> Isaiah 65:16–17

So whether you can't let go of the past because it was good or because it was bad, God wants you to know something. He knows your past. That's why He has a future for you.

> *"For I know the plans I have for you," declares the LORD, "plans to prosper you and not to harm you, plans to give you hope and a future."*
>
> Jeremiah 29:11

Notice something very significant about that verse. God's plans move beyond your past and your present.

Certainly He may use this dark experience you're going through to give you insight and sensitivity to how He's going to use you, but God's plans are based on four things.

- **God plans to prosper you.**

Interestingly, the word used here for "prosper" is *shalom,* the same word for peace. The concept is "the prosperity that comes from peace." It's a sense of assurance that all is well because God is in control. It's not about becoming wealthy; it's about becoming emotionally and spiritually healthy.

- **God plans to protect you.**

You only need protection if you are under attack. So this is not saying you are going to be problem free. Just the opposite. You are going to face adversity and distress. Life does have its battles, but God wants to protect you in those times.

- **God plans to give you hope.**

Hope is one of the most misunderstood things in the Bible. It is a powerful force that when understood and applied will make an incredible difference in your life and the lives of those you influence.

*We have this hope as an anchor for
the soul, firm and secure.*

Hebrews 6:19

Hope is a life changer. It's not wishing. It's not
an attitude. It's not positive thinking. Throughout the Bible, the concept of hope means "confident anticipation."

It's not just a state of mind; it's something that
actually influences our lifestyle. So much so that
the apostle Peter calls it a "living hope."

*Praise be to the God and Father of
our Lord Jesus Christ! In his great
mercy he has given us new birth into
a living hope through the resurrec-
tion of Jesus Christ from the dead.*

1 Peter 1:3

God's plan includes giving you this hope that
gives you confidence He is in control, and the
anticipation that He is up to something in and
through your life! Imagine living each day with
that approach to life!

- **God's plan for your life is about your
  future**.

Not about your past. Your future.

Hope means "confident anticipation."

The word for future that is used in Jeremiah 29:11 is actually the word for "the end." Isn't that odd?

However, it's not so odd when you realize what God is saying here is that His plan for you starts at the end. The end of what? The end of this darkness you are going through.

This difficulty, this sadness, this darkness is not the end. It is the page turning to a new chapter in your life.

It is ushering in a new beginning.

Dear God,
It's true, I've been holding onto the past. My life just seems to be anchored to it. But, God, I realize You have a future for me – a new beginning. Please help me to start looking to my future and Your plans for me. Help me to release my past and focus on what You want for tomorrow.

Amen

Principle #7
Find Your Ministry

What is your ministry?

What is that thing God wants to accomplish through you?

The word for ministry is "service." But here's the exciting news: it's not *your* service, it is God's service. It's what God wants to do through you!

Your ministry defines you.

> *Now I rejoice in what was suffered for you, and I fill up in my flesh what is still lacking in regard to Christ's afflictions, for the sake of his body, which is the church. I have become its servant by the commission God gave me to present to you the word of God in its fullness—the mystery that has been kept hidden for ages and generations, but is now disclosed to the saints.*
> Colossians 1:24–26

The glorious motivating truth behind Paul's ministry (he calls it his commission) was his understanding of the spiritual element of his life. It is the spiritual element of your life that truly defines you, motivates you, and determines your ministry. All of that is your "calling."

There are three basic requirements to discover your calling.

First of all, you must know your gift, ministry, and place of service.

In the same way that when you are born physically you have certain talents, when you are born spiritually you receive certain "spiritual talents." We call those spiritual gifts. The letter to the Romans defines the seven basic spiritual gifts.

> *We have different gifts, according to the grace given us. If a man's gift is prophesying, let him use it in proportion to his faith. If it is serving, let him serve; if it is teaching, let him teach; if it is encouraging, let him encourage; if it is contributing to the needs of others, let him give generously; if it is leadership, let him govern diligently; if it is showing mercy, let him do it cheerfully.*

> Romans 12:6–8

Paul describes how those gifts are to be used:

> *There are different kinds of gifts, but the same Spirit.*
>
> *There are different kinds of service, but the same Lord.*
>
> *There are different kinds of working, but the same God works all of them in all men.*
>
> 1 Corinthians 12:4–11

What we're taught here is that we have gifts and those gifts need to be used in different kinds of services (the same word for ministries); they are to be used in different "working" or places or ways of service.

The second basic requirement to accomplish your calling is that you must be motivated by God.

Where do we come up with the idea that once God impresses us with what He wants us to do, the rest is up to us? That's simply not true.

Once God has revealed the spiritual gifts He wants to use through us, He then motivates us to accomplish what He wants.

In fact, God explains it this way:

> *Delight yourself in the LORD and he will give you the desires of your heart.*
>
> Psalm 37:4

Now, most people read that verse as saying if you are delighting in God, He will give you whatever you want.

Nope. That's not what it says.

The word "delight" means to be soft and pliable. The idea is that you are seeking to please God, and whatever it takes, you are willing to do that.

When you live your life with that mindset, God promises that He will put His desires in your heart. In other words, He will motivate you to do His will.

What a great way to live your life! Your focus is on seeking to please God, and He motivates you to do His will.

Finally, you must wait on God and obey His leading and timing.

This is a tough one. We want so much for God to do something now, in our timing. However, God's timing is never in sync with our clock.

The psalmist had apparently discovered this important element concerning God's calling:

> *In the morning, O LORD, you hear my voice; in the morning I lay my requests before you and wait in expectation.*

Psalm 5:3

Wait for the LORD; be strong and take heart and wait for the LORD.
                                    Psalm 27:14

We wait in hope for the LORD; he is our help and our shield.
                                    Psalm 33:20

I wait for the LORD, my soul waits, and in his word I put my hope.
                                    Psalm 130:5

Waiting on God is one of the most difficult things we do. But the kind of waiting God wants us to do is not wasted time. Waiting on God means we are attentive and focused on Him – listening, focused, and most of all ready to do His will.

Think about this: nowhere in the Bible are we told to be busy for God.

So many Christians think they have to be busy for God. They think somehow that makes them more spiritual or acceptable to God. Interestingly, the word "busy" isn't even used favorably in the Bible.

Here is a very simple, life-changing truth: God wants to use you. He has a ministry for you. A plan He wants to accomplish through you. However, God doesn't say "Here's your assignment. Go do it."

No, what God is looking for is for you to let Him use you according to His purpose, plan, and timing. Did you get that? He wants to use you. He's not asking for you to go do "it" on your own.

You are simply a tool in God's toolbox. A hammer doesn't do its own hammering. A wrench is useless in and of itself.

One of the great discoveries you can make is that God wants to use your crisis and loss to minister to others who are dealing with issues similar to yours – maybe not exactly like yours, but similar.

God often uses the experiences of our life to define our ministry – our calling.

Why and how?

Having gone through what you did, you have a greater sensitivity to what others are dealing with.

With that in mind, let's take a look at what the Bible says about your ministry.

We are all called to specific ministries. While we may have some responsibilities in all ministry opportunities, we each have specific ministries that God has called us to accomplish.

Discovering or determining your ministry begins with understanding that you are called by God.

See, God doesn't define you by your crisis. He defines you by what He can do through you.

God doesn't define you by your crisis. He defines you by what He can do through you.

> *I press on toward the goal to win the prize for which God has called me heavenward in Christ Jesus. All of us who are mature should take such a view of things. And if on some point you think differently, that too God will make clear to you.*
>
> Philippians 3:14–15

Think about it. God has a goal for your life. This verse makes it very clear!

What? God has goals?

Absolutely!

With that in mind, let's look at this passage in Philippians and discover five things about your ministry.

- **Before you were even born, God had a goal for you!**

> *... All the days ordained for me were written in your book before one of them came to be.*
>
> Psalm 139:16

If God has a goal for you, and He knew what would happen in your life before you were even born, doesn't it make sense that what you are going through has not thwarted His intent for your life?

- **You are called to accomplish that which God put you here to do.**

This is critical to understand. You are here on earth by God's design. He has a calling on your life. No matter how badly you've messed up, or how unfocused you've been on God's plan, He still has a purpose for your life.

- **God has a prize for you at the end of the race.**

I love one of the hidden secrets of this verse. God has a prize for you regardless of where you finish in the race. He's not asking you to win, He's asking you to finish the race.

All God is asking from you is to accomplish your calling. Actually He's the one who accomplishes His calling through you. So in reality all He is asking is for you to be available to Him.

- **Your calling will end in heaven.**

While you are alive here on earth, you are called to your ministry. There is no retirement from the Christian life.

- **God will make clear what you need to know.**

You don't need to know everything involved, but God will make clear what you do need to know. This is a great way to live your life.

Many religious groups have the nonsensical idea that "you need to have enough faith" for God to work.

Can someone please explain to me what that means? The best I can figure out is that it is someone's excuse for God not doing what they wanted Him to do – apparently they didn't have enough faith.

Faith isn't about manipulating God. Faith isn't some sort of formula that controls destiny.

God doesn't expect you to know everything, or even to understand it. He simply asks you to respond to Him on the basis of what you do know.

In fact, that is the definition of faith – trusting obedience to the known will of God.

The Bible refers to a lot of people who had faith. You can find a list of many of them in Hebrews 11. However, notice that in every case the people who God says had faith already knew what God wanted them to do before they did it. They simply trusted God and obeyed what they knew.

Faith isn't about what you don't know it's about obeying and following through on what God has revealed to you.

So if you're willing and wanting to do what God wants you to do, the responsibility of making it clear to you is on God!

When my boys were young, my wife and I would give them chores. If I wanted them to clean the garage, it wasn't their responsibility to guess what I wanted them to do. It was my responsibility to make it clear what their chore was. If they were willing to do what I told them to do, but I hadn't made it clear, who was to blame?

The same is true with you and God. If your desire is to be obedient, it is God's responsibility to make His will clear.

Yes! You have a calling – a ministry. Regardless of all that has happened to you, you have a ministry. In fact, all that you've gone through will probably help to define your ministry.

I'll even take it one step further. Because of all that you've gone through, you have a greater responsibility to seek and accomplish your ministry.

Paul understood that he had a calling, a ministry, and because of that, he had a duty to perform it.

> *To be a minister of Christ Jesus to the Gentiles with the priestly duty of proclaiming the gospel of God, so that the Gentiles might become an offering acceptable to God, sanctified by the Holy Spirit.*
>
> Romans 15:16

If your desire is to be obedient, it is God's responsibility to make His will clear.

It wasn't an option. Because God called him, he had to respond. The same is true for you. Obedience to Christ is not an option that has no consequences. You either obey or you disobey. If you obey you reap the blessings of God. If you disobey, you reap the consequences of disobedience.

Once you understand that you ARE called, and you DO have a ministry that God wants to perform through you, you are empowered by the DUTY!

> *So you also, when you have done everything you were told to do, should say, "We are unworthy servants [without special merit]; we have only done our duty."*
>
> Luke 17:10

When you understand that obedience and responsiveness are not options for you, it empowers you to do what God asks of you.

> *Therefore put on the full armor of God, so that when the day of evil comes, you may be able to stand your ground, and after you have done everything, to stand.*
>
> Ephesians 6:13

Dear God,
I am overwhelmed that You want to use what I've been going through. I still don't completely understand why all this has happened, but I'm willing to turn it over to You and let You use it however You want to. God, give me the courage and sensitivity to listen and obey You. And as You reveal what You want, I am willing to obey.

Amen

Principle #8
Discover Forgiveness

You've probably heard all your life that you need to forgive people who do you wrong, or perhaps forgive yourself for an offense you committed. But why is that so important?

An unforgiven offense controls your life. By that I mean if you have not or cannot forgive a person who has wronged you, you are still somewhat controlled by that person or that offense.

The apostle Peter saw that principle in Simon's life as told in Acts 8, and he said to him:

> *For I see that you are full of bitterness and captive to sin.*
>
> Acts 8:23

A person whose sin is not forgiven is captive to that sin. It still has some control over their life.

In a similar way, if someone has committed an offense against you, if that issue hasn't been settled in your mind and heart, it still has some control over you.

That's why Jesus taught us to forgive others.

However, forgiveness is not saying, "That's okay, don't worry about it. Let's just let bygones be bygones."

For many Christians, their concept of forgiveness is similar to what happened when they were children and did something wrong and got caught.

Remember that? Your parents would say something like "Say you're sorry." So you would, and the kid you wronged would say, "That's okay," and it would be over. We grew up thinking that forgiveness is akin to feeling sorry for your sin.

Many people believe forgiveness is being sorry for your sin, and as long as God knows you're sorry for your sin, "it's okay." The result is that they spend their life feeling sorry for their sin but never discover what forgiveness is really all about.

See, forgiveness is not about sorrow. Repentance is about sorrow!

> *Godly sorrow brings repentance that leaves no regret...*
>
> 2 Corinthians 7:10

That's where confession of sin begins. It's the realization that one's sin has offended a holy and righteous God. It's the heartbreaking reality that sin caused Jesus to have to die on the cross. It's the daunting awareness that one is not right with God and needs to turn from that sin, and so confession is made to God that we're out of bounds spiritually.

That's repentance. But forgiveness is far greater than that! It's what comes after repentance.

Forgiveness is so important that Jesus included it when He taught the disciples how to pray (the Lord's Prayer):

> *This, then, is how you should pray: "Our Father in heaven, hallowed be your name, your kingdom come, your will be done on earth as it is in heaven.*
>
> *Give us today our daily bread.*
>
> *Forgive us our debts, as we also have forgiven our debtors.*
>
> *And lead us not into temptation, but deliver us from the evil one.*
>
> *For yours is the kingdom and the power and the glory forever. Amen."*
>
> Matthew 6:9–13

That's a powerful prayer Jesus taught us. It speaks to a lot of needs. And right in the middle of it is an amazing statement about forgiveness.

In fact, right after Jesus taught this prayer, He followed up with this statement:

> *For if you forgive men when they sin against you, your heavenly Father will also forgive you.*
> *But if you do not forgive men their sins, your Father will not forgive your sins.*

Matthew 6:14–15

What? Does that mean if I don't forgive someone for something horrid they did to me, I can't be forgiven for my sin?

No, not exactly.

Let's define forgiveness. To forgive literally means "to release the debt."

In a simple illustration, let's suppose you borrow some money from the bank. Once you pay it off, the bank will "release" you from the debt.

However, what if you couldn't pay it off? What if the debt was too great?

That's the situation you find yourself in because of your sin. Sin is a spiritual debt that you cannot pay off. But God has offered to release you from that debt, to forgive you. He does that because He paid the debt through Christ's death on the cross.

Sin is any offense against God. The penalty for any sin against God is eternal separation from God. The Bible calls that death.

> *For the wages of sin is death, but the gift of God is eternal life in Christ Jesus our Lord.*
>
> Romans 6:23

Because of any sin in your life, you are essentially in default. In other words, you can't pay the price for your sin and get back right with God, because even if you could die and pay the price, you would still be dead. What good would that do?

The only way out of that mess is God's mercy – His forgiveness. You need God to release you from the required penalty of your sin. That's what Jesus' death on the cross did. He paid the awful price for your sin, and in doing so He made it possible to release you from the debt of your sin.

That's why when you sin you need to let God restore that forgiveness in your life – let Him release the debt of your sin.

The price Jesus paid on the cross was so great that you can be forgiven.

Forgiveness is a process. Christ offers you forgiveness, but you have to receive it for it to be effective in your life.

Matthew 6:12 basically says that if you have received God's forgiveness for your sin, you can also forgive the person who has sinned against you.

This is an issue we have a really hard time with if we've been hurt and victimized. You may be asking yourself, "How can I forgive someone who has hurt me so badly? Does God really expect me to forgive that person who wounded me so deeply?" Let's face it, if someone really did something awful to you, more than likely there is nothing they can do to make it right, as if it never happened.

So how can you forgive someone?

We're not talking about legal issues here (although that may be included). Legal offenses are handled by the law. They have a whole different set of guidelines and requirements.

However, personal offenses are ours to forgive, ours to release. How do you do that when you've been hurt so badly?

The secret is in the little word "as."

> *Forgive us our debts, <u>as</u> we also have forgiven our debtors.*
>
> Matthew 6:12

The word "as" means "in the same way." Our forgiveness of others is to be a reflection of God's forgiveness of us.

How does that happen?

Well, God's forgiveness is based on the fact that the penalty of death for your offense against Him was paid on the cross by Jesus.

Now get this: at the very same time Jesus paid the penalty for your sin, He also paid for the sinful offense that was made against you.

Think about this:

> *God made him who had no sin to be*
> *sin for us, so that in him we might*
> *become the righteousness of God.*
> 2 Corinthians 5:21

He became sin for *us*, including the person who hurt you. In the same way that God the Father pounded your sin onto the cross, He also pounded onto the cross the sin of the person who wronged you.

If you can receive the forgiveness for your sin, you can also accept the forgiveness by God for the sin of the person who offended you. How?

Sin is being out of God's will. That's the simple definition of it.

If that person did something to you against God's will, that sin offended a holy and righteous God. We are each responsible for our own sin and acceptance of God's forgiveness. That means they need to get that settled with Him before they can

Sin is being out of God's will.

really be forgiven. But if you can accept the fact that Christ died for your sin, you can also accept the fact that He died for the sin of the person who offended you, and that is the first step in forgiving someone.

Once you recognize and believe that Christ died for that person's sin that was against you and against Him, the next step is to be willing to accept Christ's death as sufficient for their sin if they are willing to receive that.

Sometimes we are so hurt that we want the offensive person to suffer as we have, maybe more. But have you suffered as much as Christ suffered on the cross? If His suffering and dying was enough for your sin, was it not enough for the sin of the person who sinned against you?

But what about people who don't even seem to want forgiveness? What about people who just don't care that they hurt you? Are you supposed to forgive them?

Look at something Jesus taught:

> *So watch yourselves. "If your brother sins, rebuke him, and if he repents, forgive him. If he sins against you seven times in a day, and seven times comes back to you and says, 'I repent,' forgive him."*
>
> Luke 17:3–4

What Jesus is clearly saying is that if the one who has offended you repents, forgive him! If there is no repentance, there is no completed forgiveness.

The best way to explain it is that in the same way God offers forgiveness to those who will repent and receive it, we are to do the same, but it is up to the person who committed the offense to repent and seek the forgiveness.

Paul taught:

> *Bear with each other and forgive whatever grievances you may have against one another. Forgive as the Lord forgave you.*
>
> Colossians 3:13

Forgive as the Lord forgave you? How did He do that? He forgave you when you repented and went to Him for His forgiveness. His willingness has always been there to forgive because the price He paid was so great.

In the same way, when you realize God loves that person who hurt you, and that He died for them too and is willing to forgive them if they repent, you also can "release the debt" of their sin if they repent. After all, the Christ who died for you also died for them.

For those who have been deeply hurt by others and have not been able to forgive them:

Dear God,
I have been hurt so deeply that there is no way to describe my pain. Someone's sin has hurt me beyond expression. By Your own word you state that this person (these people) deserve eternal torment in hell.

Yet, I understand that my own sin caused incredible pain to Jesus on the cross. And in fact, I deserve hell also. But by your grace and mercy, You have forgiven me. Teach me to forgive like that. And should they ask for my forgiveness, give me the grace to show your mercy.

I ask you to show this person (these people) how terrible their sin has been against you and against me. Cause them to have great regret and remorse. Even cause them to repent of what they have done. Create in them such a sense of sorrow that they would cry out to You for mercy and forgiveness.

I acknowledge that You are the eternal judge, not me.

God, I put these people behind me so that there is nothing between You and me.

Amen

For those who have not been able to forgive themselves because of their own sin:

> *Dear God,*
> *I struggle to come before You to ask forgiveness. My sin is so disgusting and disturbing that I deserve your eternal punishment. But your Word teaches that when Jesus was brutally beaten, tortured and killed, it was for my sin. You planned ahead, thinking of my sin when you allowed Jesus to die because of it on the cross. That death was the most horrific, painful and degrading death that one could die, and He did that for me.*
>
> *I will no longer refuse to accept that His death wasn't enough for my sin. I will no longer deny that You really do love me, even though I have trouble understanding that. I will not insult you by acting like you did not suffer enough to forgive my sin.*
>
> *You are my judge, and You have ruled that I was forgiven at the cross. I receive that forgiveness. I will no longer refuse to forgive myself, as if my moral standards were higher than You.*

I am no longer worthless; I am forgiven.

I am no longer damaged goods; I am forgiven.

I am no longer useless; I am forgiven.

I am no longer rejected; I am forgiven.

God, please continue to work in my life to accomplish what You want.

Amen

Principle #9
Laugh Again

This is unquestionably one of the most practical yet life-changing things you can discover. And it's so biblical!

> *Our mouths were filled with laughter, our tongues with songs of joy. Then it was said among the nations, "The LORD has done great things for them."*
>
> Psalm 126:2

> *There is a time for everything, and a season for every activity under heaven...a time to weep and a time to laugh...*
>
> Ecclesiastes 3:1,4

> *She is clothed with strength and dignity; she can laugh at the days to come.*
>
> Proverbs 31:25

We've referred several times to the life of Abraham. One of the things I love about Abraham is his sense of humor.

> *Abraham fell facedown; he laughed and said to himself, "Will a son be born to a man a hundred years old? Will Sarah bear a child at the age of ninety?"*

Genesis 17:17

I don't think Abraham was questioning God. I suspect he was just taking an honest look at his life and recognizing that he was not fathering material. It wasn't an affront against God, it was a simple realization that he was old and beyond his daddy years—by man's standards.

Interestingly, Sarah seemed to have that same sense of humor.

For years I read and studied the story of Abraham and Sarah with the understanding that when they laughed they were secretly doubting God, even laughing at God. Now I'm sure that was not the case. In fact, even if it were, there was a turning point when God came to Abraham and told him that within a year he would have a son through Sarah. The Bible says that Sarah overheard and laughed.

Then there was a strange moment when God asked why Sarah was laughing (as if He didn't know).

Sarah was afraid, so she lied and said, "I did not laugh." But He said, "Yes, you did laugh."

Genesis 18:15

Awkward!

You need to understand something about Sarah.

Sarah was considered a cultural disgrace. She was barren, and in that society your worth as a woman was measured by your ability to bear children. After all, didn't God command them to *"be fruitful and multiply and fill the earth?"* (Genesis 9:7)

Abraham had every societal right to dump her. No one would have thought less of him for it. She was, after all, dead wood. She had nothing to contribute as far as society was concerned.

Sarah even thought of herself that way. When God told her she was going to get pregnant, she laughed because she knew how worthless she was. She was a loser. She was barren. She was old. And she knew it. We would call her "damaged goods." That's all she was as far as society was concerned.

But God had other plans. Sarah saw herself as worthless, but God saw her as part of His plan. Sarah would get pregnant, but not until she was where God wanted her.

For this was how the promise was stated: "At the appointed time I will return, and Sarah will have a son."

Romans 9:9

God took someone who was considered worthless...without value...and changed the world.

Listen to me, you who pursue righteousness and who seek the LORD: Look to the rock from which you were cut and to the quarry from which you were hewn; look to Abraham, your father, and to Sarah, who gave you birth. When I called him he was but one, and I blessed him and made him many.

Isaiah 51:1–2

You may not see yourself as worth much or of any particular value to God. You may see yourself as damaged goods or a cultural disgrace, but God sees you differently, and He's ready to pour out His grace – His unmerited favor – on you...at the right time, in the right place.

A few months later when Sarah realized that everything God said was coming true, she made a most enlightening statement:

*God has brought me laughter, and
everyone who hears about this will
laugh with me.*

Genesis 21:6

Did you catch that? Sarah realized that in spite
of how intense, serious, and life-changing the
birth of Isaac was, there was also something hu-
morous about it—she was ninety years old! More
importantly, God was in control and had given
her the insight to laugh.

She could laugh at the circumstances but be
totally serious about the fact that her life was
changing drastically.

As we saw back in the third principle, Probabilities Versus Possibilities, joy is actually
"brightness." It is the sense of light coming into
the darkness of your life. Now think about this:
humor is the window that lets the light of joy into
your darkness.

Finding humor in some of the oddities and in-
congruent things of life helps you begin to see
things in the light of joy.

A few months ago I officiated a funeral for a
woman from a very large family. She had four
children and was an aunt to many more. Her
passing was quite sudden and certainly very
sad. One of her remarkable characteristics was
her sheer joy in life. She loved to laugh. Every

Humor is the window
that lets the light of joy
into your darkness.

day seemed to be a great experience for her. She made people around her feel that way, and it was evident in the way people remembered her.

The family gathered around the casket after the service. They stood there silently, awkwardly, not knowing what to say or do. Finally one of her daughters said quietly, "If she knew we were burying her in that dress, she would just die!"

Suddenly a ripple of giggles moved through the group. Then more giggles. Then laughter. And tears. And smiles. And hugs. And more tears. And somehow through that, an affirmation that they were still family and still had each other.

When you're hurting and grieving, it's okay to give yourself permission to find humor and laugh again, to let the light of joy shine in on your life once more.

Humor gives you balance. When your life has been so focused on the difficult and sad matters at hand, you need to give yourself the freedom to escape to another emotion, an emotion that God created. Let yourself laugh, and find the balance that you need.

> *Blessed are you who weep now, for you will laugh.*
>
> Luke 6:21

My friend David Naster, a comedian who has written several books that begin their title with "You Just Have to Laugh...," made this brilliant observation: "Enjoying the absurdity of life's incongruities is the only weapon we have against the paralysis of our emotions. When we laugh during turbulent times the uphill road isn't as steep because emotions aren't weighing us down."

Laugh again!

It may take a little time before you're ready for that, but when you feel that little crinkle in the corner of your mouth, in spite of the pain you've been going through, go ahead...let it go.

And if you find yourself laughing and crying at the same time, it's okay. It's a step toward healing.

> *Dear God,*
> *It's been so long since I've found humor in anything. I really don't feel like laughing. I'm hurting so deeply! God, give me some balance. Help me find some humor in my life.*
>
> *Amen*

Principle #10
Live For A New Day

New days mean new opportunities, new options, new discoveries, new goals, new accomplishments, and sometimes new conflicts. If we drag the old day into the new day, it just complicates matters. While we still have to live with the consequences of the old day, the new day gives us another chance to overcome those consequences.

> *Weeping may remain for a night, but rejoicing comes in the morning.*
>
> Psalm 30:5

One of the greatest lessons I've learned in my life concerns the circumstances of my life.

- **Circumstances develop the character of your life.**
- **Character determines the choices for your life.**

- **Choices define the consequences in your life.**

You may not be able to change the circumstances of your life, but if you have the right character you will make the right choices. Then the right choices will define the consequences in your life. And the right consequences will overcome the wrong circumstances of your life!

Start focusing on a new day where you are no longer controlled by the circumstances of your life, but rather you control the consequences because you make the right choices.

The point of this principle is that you need to define your future, not by your current circumstances, but by the consequences that develop because of the choices you make. And those choices need to be within the context of God's plans.

One thing is clear from the Bible: God intends for you to have a new day. Not one that is about you. One that is about Him.

> *...Every new day he does not fail.*
> Zephaniah 3:5

I love the hidden truth in this verse. The new day is about God, not you. It's about what He accomplishes, not you. It's about His success, not yours.

What an amazing truth! God is not dwelling on your failures or flaws. He's looking ahead to a new day through your life.

The New Day principle is a critically important one in the Bible. The first time we encounter it is in the life of Noah.

Noah was in the ark for a little over a year. Finally the ark came to rest on dry land, and after a few days Noah was able to step out onto dry ground.

The first thing he did was build an altar, a place to worship God.

> *Then Noah built an altar to the LORD and, taking some of all the clean animals and clean birds, he sacrificed burnt offerings on it.*
>
> Genesis 8:20

One of the significant things about this is that an altar is a marker – a place where one meets God and then moves on!

The pagan ritual was to build an altar and keep coming back to it. But every time an altar was built to worship God in the Bible, it was a place and time where one met God and then moved on. Even if they came back to it at some point, it was still a place that marked where they had met God and then moved on. Even in the Jewish temple,

An altar is a marker – a place where one meets God and then moves on!

once you sacrificed on the altar, you were to move on past the altar to fellowship with God.

So the New Day principle is that you must meet God and then move on with life.

> *So I say, "My splendor is gone and all that I had hoped from the LORD."*
>
> *I remember my affliction and my wandering, the bitterness and the gall.*
>
> *I well remember them, and my soul is downcast within me.*
>
> *Yet this I call to mind and therefore I have hope:*
>
> *Because of the Lord's great love we are not consumed, for his compassions never fail.*
>
> *They are new every morning; great is your faithfulness.*
>
> Lamentations 3:18–23

However, there is one important thing to note. Start your new day today. Don't put it off until another time, another day. Start now. In the darkness.

When I was a boy, my dad sometimes took me with him on mission trips into the Honduran jungles. I loved those adventures and was always eager to go.

One particular journey was going to be a long one. It would take a few days to get to our destination, a little mountaintop village. It meant that we needed as much daylight as we could get for the journey.

My dad woke me up in what seemed to be the middle of the night and told me to get ready to leave.

"What?" I mumbled. "It's still dark!"

"Oh, that would explain why you're asleep," he teased. "We've got to get up and get going in the dark so we can do what we have to do in the light."

It's a significant truth.

You may be in the darkness right now. But don't wait for a new day to break before you start planning for it. The later you start, the less time you'll have. Get up and get going.

Here are five things you need to do in your darkness to get ready for the new day.

- **Acknowledge the presence of God in your darkness.**

He who dwells in the shelter of the Most High will rest in the shadow of the Almighty.

I will say of the LORD, "He is my refuge and my fortress, my God, in whom I trust."

Surely he will save you from the fowler's snare and from the deadly pestilence.

He will cover you with his feathers, and under his wings you will find refuge; his faithfulness will be your shield and rampart.

You will not fear the terror of night...

Psalm 91:1–5

Sometimes it's hard to believe that God is with us in the darkness.

When my boys were very small we lived quite a distance from our parents, so we traveled as often as possible to visit them.

On one trip we stayed in a motel where the room was very dark. After we had put the boys to bed and turned the lights out, Eric, my oldest, timidly whispered, "Dad?"

"Yes?"

"I just wanted to know you're there."

We need that kind of relationship with God.

You may not be able to see God in your darkness, but you need to know He's there.

Spend some time talking to Him. Ask Him to let you know He's there with you.

- **Make sure you're right with God even in your darkness.**

  Though you probe my heart and examine me at night, though you test me, you will find nothing; I have resolved that my mouth will not sin.

  Psalm 17:3

Just because things have not gone well in your life is no reason to neglect your relationship with God. If anything, it is a greater reason to connect with God.

In order for God to work in your life, you need to make sure you are right with Him, that the channels of communication are open and clear of sin.

Sin distorts what God says to us. In fact, it often completely blocks it.

Confess your sin to Him; make it right. And listen to God in the darkness.

- **Learn to worship in the darkness**

  On my bed I remember you; I think of you through the watches of the night.
  Because you are my help, I sing in the shadow of your wings.

  Psalm 63:6–7

I love what this verse implies: start where you are. If you are so beaten down, and so weak that you barely have enough strength to even just think about God, start there. And when you find yourself unable to sleep, or constantly waking up, think about God.

Before long you'll find yourself understanding more about God, and that will lead to a greater appreciation of Him in your life. You'll begin to see His help in your life, and you'll start worshipping Him even if it's just from a distance.

But eventually, when the darkness and distress hits, you'll find yourself going right to God.

Why?

Because you'll know He's there.

> *When I was in distress, I sought the Lord; at night I stretched out untiring hands and my soul refused to be comforted....I remembered my songs in the night.*
>
> Psalm 77:2,6

- **Listen to God in your darkness**

> *I will praise the LORD, who counsels me; even at night my heart instructs me.*
>
> Psalm 16:7

It's so easy when you're in the darkness to see nothing but darkness. When all you see is darkness, you associate all you hear with darkness. But God is speaking, even in the darkness.

The more time you spend with Him, the more you'll get to know His voice and understand Him.

> *My sheep listen to my voice; I know them, and they follow me.*
>
> John 10:27

- **Meet God in the darkness.**

This is such an important point. You need to meet God in the crisis, not after the crisis is over. Over and over we are given this truth in the Word of God.

Where did Jacob meet God? In the darkness!

> *That night Jacob got up and took his two wives, his two maidservants and his eleven sons and crossed the ford of the Jabbok. After he had sent them across the stream, he sent over all his possessions. So Jacob was left alone, and a man wrestled with him till daybreak.*
>
> Genesis 32:22–24

Where did Moses meet God? In the darkness!

> *Moses said to the people, "Do not be*
> *afraid. God has come to test you,*
> *so that the fear of God will be with*
> *you to keep you from sinning." The*
> *people remained at a distance, while*
> *Moses approached the thick dark-*
> *ness where God was.*
>
> Exodus 20:20–11

Where did Elijah meet God? In the darkness!

> *There he went into a cave and spent*
> *the night. And the word of the LORD*
> *came to him: "What are you doing*
> *here, Elijah?"*
>
> 1 Kings 19:9

And the symbolism goes on and on.

Where did the shepherds meet God? In the darkness!

> *And there were shepherds living out*
> *in the fields nearby, keeping watch*
> *over their flocks at night. An angel of*
> *the Lord appeared to them, and the*
> *glory of the Lord shone around them,*
> *and they were terrified....When the*

angels had left them and gone into heaven, the shepherds said to one another, "Let's go to Bethlehem and see this thing that has happened, which the Lord has told us about." So they hurried off and found Mary and Joseph, and the baby, who was lying in the manger.

Luke 2:8–16

Where did Paul discover God? In the darkness of his blindness!

He fell to the ground and heard a voice say to him, "Saul, Saul, why do you persecute me?"....Saul got up from the ground, but when he opened his eyes he could see nothing. So they led him by the hand into Damascus. For three days he was blind, and did not eat or drink anything.

Acts 9:4–9

When did Jesus die on the cross? In the darkness!

It was now about the sixth hour, and darkness came over the whole land until the ninth hour, for the sun stopped shining. And the curtain of the temple was torn in two. Jesus called out with a loud voice, "Father, into your hands I commit my spirit." When he had said this, he breathed his last.

Luke 23:44–46

When did Jesus rise from the tomb? In the darkness!

Very early on the first day of the week, just after sunrise, they were on their way to the tomb and they asked each other, "Who will roll the stone away from the entrance of the tomb?" But when they looked up, they saw that the stone, which was very large, had been rolled away. As they entered the tomb, they saw a young man dressed in a white robe sitting on the right side, and they were alarmed. "Don't be alarmed," he said. "You are looking for Jesus the Nazarene, who was crucified. He has risen!"

Mark 16:2–16

You can meet God in your darkness.

*It is good to praise the LORD and
make music to your name, O Most
High,to proclaim your love in the
morning and your faithfulness at
night.*

Psalm 92:1–2

And once you've met God in the darkness, you'll
be ready for the new day.

If you focus on the darkness of your life, and
concentrate on how to survive the night, that's
what you'll still be doing when the new day
breaks.

Yes, you've got to get through the night before
the new day starts, but you have a choice. You
can either focus on how dark it is or plan for how
light it will soon be.

*Satisfy us in the morning with your
unfailing love, that we may sing for
joy and be glad all our days.*

Psalm 90:14

*Dear God,
This is a tough one to learn. I want a
new day in my life, but it's sometimes
tough to move past today and plan
for tomorrow. Help me to see beyond
now. Help me to understand that*

You can either focus on how dark it is or plan for how light it will soon be.

You have made plans for tomorrow that I don't even know about. Give me the courage to reach for a new tomorrow and move on with my life.

Amen

Principle #11
Begin To Worship

---

*Shout for joy to the LORD, all the
earth.*

*Worship the LORD with gladness;
come before him with joyful songs.*

*Know that the LORD is God. It is
he who made us, and we are his; we
are his people, the sheep of his pas-
ture.*

*Enter his gates with thanksgiv-
ing and his courts with praise; give
thanks to him and praise his name.*

*For the LORD is good and his love
endures forever; his faithfulness con-
tinues through all generations.*

Psalm 100

Worship changes everything. Discovering worship changes life. It opens up the channels of
communication with God. It puts our focus where

it needs to be. And it puts our problems and conflicts where they need to be.

Worship isn't about ignoring your problems but rather seeing them from a bigger perspective, with a greater understanding.

But what IS worship?

Worship is absolute surrender to the holiness of God and all the demands that makes on my life.

To understand worship, it is important to first look at what it is not.

- **Worship is not religious activity**

Jesus made this point very clear:

> *He replied, "Isaiah was right when he prophesied about you hypocrites; as it is written: 'These people honor me with their lips, but their hearts are far from me.*
>
> *They worship me in vain; their teachings are but rules taught by men.'*
>
> *You have let go of the commands of God and are holding on to the traditions of men."*
>
> *And he said to them: "You have*

a fine way of setting aside the commands of God in order to observe your own traditions!"

Mark 7:6–9 (quoting Isaiah 29:13)

• Worship is not defined by style

In today's church it seems we feel a need to define worship by style, such as contemporary worship, or jazz worship, or sacred worship, or even blended worship.

However, worship is not about style. But make no mistake: God does care about how we worship Him!

Look at Leviticus 10:

> *Aaron's sons Nadab and Abihu took their censers, put fire in them and added incense; and they offered unauthorized fire before the LORD, contrary to his command. So fire came out from the presence of the LORD and consumed them, and they died before the LORD. Moses then said to Aaron, "This is what the LORD spoke of when he said: 'Among those who approach me I will show myself holy; in the sight of all the people I will be honored.'"*

Aaron remained silent. Moses summoned Mishael and Elzaphan, sons of Aaron's uncle Uzziel, and said to them, "Come here; carry your cousins outside the camp, away from the front of the sanctuary." So they came and carried them, still in their tunics, outside the camp, as Moses ordered. Then Moses said to Aaron and his sons Eleazar and Ithamar, "Do not let your hair become unkempt, and do not tear your clothes, or you will die and the LORD will be angry with the whole community. But your relatives, all the house of Israel, may mourn for those the LORD has destroyed by fire. Do not leave the entrance to the Tent of Meeting or you will die, because the Lord's anointing oil is on you." So they did as Moses said. Then the LORD said to Aaron, "You and your sons are not to drink wine or other fermented drink whenever you go into the Tent of Meeting, or you will die. This is a lasting ordinance for the generations to come. You must distinguish between the holy and the common, between the unclean and the clean,

*and you must teach the Israelites
all the decrees the LORD has given
them through Moses."*

Leviticus 10:1–11

Worship is very important to God. He takes it
very seriously. When people become bored with
worship or make worship about satisfying themselves, He is offended.

Look at what God says in Malachi:

> *"A son honors his father, and a ser-
> vant his master. If I am a father,
> where is the honor due me? If I am
> a master, where is the respect due
> me?" says the LORD Almighty. "It is
> you, O priests, who show contempt
> for my name. But you ask, 'How have
> we shown contempt for your name?'
> You place defiled food on my altar.
> But you ask, 'How have we defiled
> you?' By saying that the Lord's ta-
> ble is contemptible. When you bring
> blind animals for sacrifice, is that
> not wrong? When you sacrifice crip-
> pled or diseased animals, is that not
> wrong? Try offering them to your
> governor! Would he be pleased with
> you? Would he accept you?" says the*

LORD Almighty. "Now implore God to be gracious to us. With such offerings from your hands, will he accept you?"—says the LORD Almighty. "Oh, that one of you would shut the temple doors, so that you would not light useless fires on my altar! I am not pleased with you," says the LORD Almighty, "and I will accept no offering from your hands. My name will be great among the nations, from the rising to the setting of the sun. In every place incense and pure offerings will be brought to my name, because my name will be great among the nations," says the LORD Almighty. "But you profane it by saying of the Lord's table, 'It is defiled,' and of its food, 'It is contemptible.' And you say, 'What a burden!' and you sniff at it contemptuously," says the LORD Almighty. "When you bring injured, crippled or diseased animals and offer them as sacrifices, should I accept them from your hands?" says the LORD. "Cursed is the cheat who has an acceptable male in his flock and vows to give it, but then

*sacrifices a blemished animal to
the Lord. For I am a great king,"
says the LORD Almighty, "and my
name is to be feared among the nations....And now this admonition is
for you, O priests. If you do not listen, and if you do not set your heart
to honor my name," says the LORD
Almighty, "I will send a curse upon
you, and I will curse your blessings.
Yes, I have already cursed them, because you have not set your heart to
honor me."*

Malachi 1:6–2:2

- **Worship is not motions and emotions**

It's not about big stirring music and special
lighting.

It's not about praise choruses or old hymns.

It's not about saying certain prayers.

It's not about the preacher stepping on your
toes.

It's not about how many people made public
decisions.

It's not about the doxology and saying the
Lord's Prayer and Communion.

It's not about feeling motivated or uplifted.

It's not about feeling the Spirit.

True worship does not mistake:

Contentment for Commitment
    Enthusiasm for Obedience
        Conviction for Brokenness
            Laughter for Joy
                Resolve for Renewal

Jesus quoted Isaiah against people who define worship by what satisfies them.

> *He replied, "Isaiah was right when he prophesied about you hypocrites; as it is written: 'These people honor me with their lips, but their hearts are far from me. They worship me in vain; their teachings are but rules taught by men.' You have let go of the commands of God and are holding on to the traditions of men." And he said to them: "You have a fine way of setting aside the commands of God in order to observe your own traditions!"*
>
> Mark 7:6–9

So what is worship?

Jesus defined it in the passage we just looked at in Mark.

• Worship is about obeying God

In fact, Jesus made this very clear.

> *Why do you call me, 'Lord, Lord,'*
> *and do not do what I say?*
>
> Luke 6:46

The term "Lord, Lord" was probably a reference to something that was said in temple worship. What Jesus was asking was, "Why do you go through the motions, but when it comes down to the reality, you don't obey me?"

• Worship is about pleasing God

Pleasing Him by getting right with Him. Pleasing Him by sharing your life with Him. Pleasing Him by depending on Him.

> *May the God of peace, who through the*
> *blood of the eternal covenant brought*
> *back from the dead our Lord Jesus, that*
> *great Shepherd of the sheep, equip you*
> *with everything good for doing his will,*
> *and may he work in us what is pleasing*
> *to him, through Jesus Christ, to whom*
> *be glory for ever and ever. Amen.*
>
> Hebrews 13:20–21

- **Worship requires surrender**

Worship that doesn't demand a change in your life is not worship, it's just entertainment. Worship that doesn't require surrender is not worship.

> *Splendor and majesty are before him; strength and joy in his dwelling place. Ascribe to the LORD, O families of nations, ascribe to the LORD glory and strength, ascribe to the LORD the glory due his name. Bring an offering and come before him; worship the LORD in the splendor of his holiness.*
>
> 1 Chronicles 16:27–29

> *Ascribe to the LORD the glory due his name; worship the LORD in the splendor of his holiness.*
>
> Psalm 29:2

> *Worship the LORD in the splendor of his holiness; tremble before him, all the earth.*
>
> Psalm 96:9

Isaiah had that sort of worship experience and talked about it:

In the year that King Uzziah died, I saw the Lord seated on a throne, high and exalted, and the train of his robe filled the temple.

Above him were seraphs, each with six wings: With two wings they covered their faces, with two they covered their feet, and with two they were flying.

And they were calling to one another: "Holy, holy, holy is the LORD Almighty; the whole earth is full of his glory."

At the sound of their voices the doorposts and thresholds shook and the temple was filled with smoke.

"Woe to me!" I cried. "I am ruined! For I am a man of unclean lips, and I live among a people of unclean lips, and my eyes have seen the King, the LORD Almighty."

Isaiah 6:1–5

Isaiah encountered the holiness of God and was never the same again. And that encounter required his total surrender and response to the will of God.

That is worship!

For you are great and do marvelous deeds; you alone are God.

Teach me your way, O LORD, and I will walk in your truth; give me an undivided heart, that I may fear your name.

Psalm 86:10–11

So if we define worship as absolute surrender to the holiness of God and all the demands that makes on your life, then it requires that you spend time with God, receiving His direction, seeking His will, and committing yourself to His desire and call for your life—even now while your life is shattered.

Dear God,
I'm discovering that worship is not about my likes or dislikes, but about You. I always thought worship was about making me feel something. Lord, I'm realizing that life is not about me. It's about You. Would You please give me the wisdom, courage, and strength to live out what You want, not what I want.

Amen

Where Do I Begin?

I don't want to oversimplify this, but if you're wondering how and where you start putting your life back together, the answer is simple: start at the point of your need.

Why? Because that's where God is at work. God is in the business of meeting needs. That's what He does. He's not out to bless your abundance. He's out to meet your needs. So if you want to know what God is up to in your life, look at the needs in your life.

The Scriptures are very clear on this:

> *And my God will meet all your needs according to his glorious riches in Christ Jesus.*
>
> Philippians 4:19

> *The LORD protects the simplehearted; when I was in great need, he saved me.*
>
> Psalm 116:6

And God is able to make all grace abound to you, so that in all things at all times, having all that you need, you will abound in every good work.

2 Corinthians 9:8

His divine power has given us everything we need for life and godliness through our knowledge of him who called us by his own glory and goodness.

2 Peter 1:3

Let us then approach the throne of grace with confidence, so that we may receive mercy and find grace to help us in our time of need.

Hebrews 4:16

This is really important. Just because you know your needs doesn't mean it is up to you to solve them. When our dreams have been broken and our lives are shattered, that's often right where we find God in a fresh and life-changing way.

I love to study the life of Jacob. Here's a guy who would've fit in well in the world today. He was a schemer and a deceiver. He had even deceived his old blind father into giving him the family inheritance instead of passing it along to his older brother as was the custom.

Then, years later, something happened. He found out that his brother, Esau, was coming for him, and he went into crisis mode.

Now, we all have times of crisis in our lives. The way most of us handle crisis is exactly the way Jacob did.

First, we look for an escape.

> *In great fear and distress Jacob divided the people who were with him into two groups, and the flocks and herds and camels as well. He thought, "If Esau comes and attacks one group, the group that is left may escape."*

Genesis 32:7–8

Then we start Panic Praying.

> *Then Jacob prayed, "O God of my father Abraham, God of my father Isaac, O LORD, who said to me, 'Go back to your country and your relatives, and I will make you prosper,' I am unworthy of all the kindness and faithfulness you have shown your servant. I had only my staff*

> *when I crossed this Jordan, but now*
> *I have become two groups. Save me,*
> *I pray, from the hand of my brother*
> *Esau, for I am afraid he will come*
> *and attack me, and also the moth-*
> *ers with their children. But you have*
> *said, 'I will surely make you prosper*
> *and will make your descendants like*
> *the sand of the sea, which cannot be*
> *counted.'"*
>
> Genesis 32:9–12

Notice the tone of Jacob's prayer – me, me, me. It's all about me. Not only that, but he even tries to manipulate God with the old "Wait a minute, God, You said…You promised." It's like Jacob believed God owed him something.

Panic praying is all about trying to control the situation. It's not really about trusting God; it's about controlling God – making deals with Him. That leads to the next dangerous step: scheming.

For the Christian, this is our Plan B. In the back of our minds we're hoping God will come through and save us from the crisis, but if He doesn't, then we feel we've got to put a plan together. You know, just in case. And we start scheming.

That's exactly what Jacob did right after he prayed that God would deliver him.

He spent the night there, and from what he had with him he selected a gift for his brother Esau: two hundred female goats and twenty male goats, two hundred ewes and twenty rams, thirty female camels with their young, forty cows and ten bulls, and twenty female donkeys and ten male donkeys.

He put them in the care of his servants, each herd by itself, and said to his servants, "Go ahead of me, and keep some space between the herds."

He instructed the one in the lead: "When my brother Esau meets you and asks, 'To whom do you belong, and where are you going, and who owns all these animals in front of you?' then you are to say, 'They belong to your servant Jacob. They are a gift sent to my lord Esau, and he is coming behind us.'"

He also instructed the second, the third and all the others who followed the herds: "You are to say the same thing to Esau when you meet him.

And be sure to say, 'Your servant Jacob is coming behind us.'" For he thought, "I will pacify him with

> *these gifts I am sending on ahead;*
> *later, when I see him, perhaps he*
> *will receive me."*
>
> Genesis 32:13–20

Then when things still don't seem to go right, and we don't see God working, and we can't figure out anything else to do, we give up.

> *So Jacob's gifts went on ahead of*
> *him, but he himself spent the night*
> *in the camp.*
> *   That night Jacob got up and took*
> *his two wives, his two maidservants,*
> *and his eleven sons and crossed the*
> *ford of the Jabbok.*
> *   After he had sent them across the*
> *stream, he sent over all his posses-*
> *sions.*
>
> Genesis 32:21–23

It's in our darkest moment, when all seems lost, that God shows up—but almost never the way we expect Him to. In fact, at first He seemed like another problem for Jacob, a man who came to fight him.

Jacob wanted God to solve the problem in a way that made sense to him. He wanted God to fix the circumstances.

It's in our darkest moment, when all seems lost, that God shows up—but almost never the way we expect Him

God was going to bring about a solution, but not according to Jacob's plan.

To Jacob, solving the problem would have put an end to the mess, and then he could get on with his life. To God, solving the problem was just the beginning of what He wanted to do.

> *So Jacob was left alone, and a man*
> *wrestled with him till daybreak.*
>
> Genesis 32:24

It was at this point that Jacob realized his reality: there was nothing he could do to win. No amount of scheming or deception would get him out of this predicament. He had lost everything. He desperately needed God's blessing.

That's when he met God in the crisis.

So you are in a crisis now. Something has gone terribly wrong in your life and you need to find a way to pick up the pieces and mend your heart. What should you do next?

Let me suggest you learn from Jacob and what he did at the darkest point of his life.

- **Seek the blessing of God**

> *Then the man said, "Let me go, for*
> *it is daybreak." But Jacob replied, "I*

will not let you go unless you bless me."

Genesis 32:26

The word "blessing" throughout the Bible means "that which causes one to praise and adore God."

If someone blesses you, it means they do something that causes you to praise God. If you bless someone, it means you cause them to praise God. When God blesses you, it does the same thing—it causes you to praise and adore Him.

Ask God to bless you! Ask Him to do something in your life that will cause you to praise Him!

The fact is God really does want to bless you.

...see if I will not throw open the floodgates of heaven and pour out so much blessing that you will not have room enough for it.

Malachi 3:10

...to this you were called so that you may inherit a blessing.

1 Peter 3:9

Notice this blessing principle:

[God]...turned the curse into a bless-

ing for you, because the LORD your
God loves you.

Deuteronomy 23:5

Start by asking God to somehow turn your broken dreams and your shattered life into a blessing.

- **Allow God to transform you**

  The man asked him, "What is your
  name?" "Jacob," he answered. Then
  the man said, "Your name will no
  longer be Jacob, but Israel, because
  you have struggled with God and
  with men and have overcome."

  Genesis 32:27–28

This is such an amazing thing God does. Whenever God changed someone's name, He did it to define their ministry. He did it with Abraham, Sarah, Jacob, Peter, and even Paul. In every case the change came after a critical time in their lives, a time of struggle and great difficulty.

The idea here is that God will give you a new sense of identity through your experience – a fresh insight to your destiny, what He wants to do in and through your life...even after your life is over here on earth!

God is in the business of change. Sometimes He causes it. Sometimes He allows it. But in every case, He has something He wants to accomplish through it. So, as your world has changed, let God change you, transform you, to accomplish what He wants to do in and through you.

- **Yield to the authority of God**

> *Jacob said, "Please tell me your name." But he replied, "Why do you ask my name?" Then he blessed him there.*
>
> Genesis 32:29

It was a very strange question, and an even stranger response.

In that culture and in most cultures, a person's name is of extreme importance. A name is one's identity. In the same way that the word "chair" identifies a certain object, one's name identifies a person, and we associate all the characteristics, talents, and abilities that person has with their name.

For example, when I say Abraham Lincoln, you might think of him as the president, or the Great Emancipator, or a tall man with a beard. His name encompasses all that he is. If I say Albert Einstein, many of you think genius. Some think of E=mc². Some think of wild hair. But his name encompasses all that he is.

What Jacob was asking was, "Who are you so that I can know what you do."

And God's answer was amazing – *"Why do you ask my name?"*

God was telling Jacob (and us) to quit playing games. He was saying "don't say you want to know Me and claim My name if you aren't willing to follow and obey Me." He said it this way in Isaiah:

> *I am the LORD: <u>that is my name</u>! I will not give my glory to another or my praise to idols!*
>
> Isaiah 42:8

If you've been playing games, pretending about your relationship with God, it's time to get serious. Get to know God. Yield to His unquestioned authority in your life. You're part of a higher calling than you've ever imagined. God is up to eternal work through your life. Let Him have His way.

Apparently that is exactly what Jacob did, because Genesis 32:29 says that God blessed Jacob.

Then something very curious happened to Jacob.

*The sun rose above him as he passed
Peniel, and he was limping because
of his hip.*

Genesis 32:31

Notice the principle we saw in Principle 10 –
Live for a New Day: *"The sun rose..."* But there
was something else: *"...and he was limping..."*

This is so important to catch. After you meet
God in the crisis you will always walk with a
limp – you will never be the same. There will always be something left to remind you of the time
God met you in the darkness and brought you
through the crisis. It is a reminder that God is in
control and has a plan for your life.

You have been through so much. Your life will never be the same. But the good news is that God is there in your darkness to bring you into a new day.

It is impossible to see everything that God is up to, but He is at work. He has eternal plans for you.

A few years ago I was in south Missouri teaching a seminar on knowing God's will. In one of the sessions I focused on the fact that God is not finished with us. As long as we are alive God is at work.

After the session, an old farmer came up to me and asked, "Do you really believe that?"

"Uh...yeah, I'm pretty sure I believe what I said. What in particular are you referring to?"

"I mean, do you really think God can use someone that has ignored Him all his life?"

"God's pretty patient!"

"You mean, if you ain't dead, God ain't done?"

I couldn't have said it any better.

—⁓—

Hasten, O God, to save me; O LORD, come quickly to help me.

May those who seek my life be put to shame and confusion; may all who desire my ruin be turned back in disgrace.

May those who say to me, "Aha! Aha!" turn back because of their shame.

But may all who seek you rejoice and be glad in you; may those who love your salvation always say, "Let God be exalted!"

Yet I am poor and needy; come quickly to me, O God. You are my help and my deliverer; O LORD, do not delay.

Psalm 70

About the Author

Dan Hurst is the lead teacher for The Open Class, a Bible study he started at First Baptist Church of Raytown, Missouri. The class has several hundred members.

As the son of missionary parents to Honduras, he grew up in a culture of ministry based on teaching God's Word in a way that can be understood practically and applied. Many of those principles carried over to his ministry efforts as a Bible teacher.

Dan and his wife, Marcia, live in the Kansas City area. Although his business, conference speaking, and teaching keep him busy, he finds time to ruin some golf courses and cheer on losing sports teams.

To contact Dan Hurst:

www.LivingPower.com

(660) 851–1510